October

# We survived ... At last I speak.

Leon Malmed

To : Michel

Thank you for your interest.

Leon Malmed

*Tree planted at Yad Vashem Memorial in Jerusalem in honor of the Righteous Henri and Suzanne Ribouleau*

# We survived

...

# At last I speak

Leon Malmed

Zea Books
Lincoln, Nebraska
2013

ISBN 978-1-60962-026-4 paperback
ISBN 978-1-60962-027-1 e-book

Set in Constantia types.
Design and composition by Paul Royster.

Zea Books are published by the
University of Nebraska–Lincoln Libraries.

Electronic (pdf) edition available online at
http://digitalcommons.unl.edu/zeabook/14/
Print edition can be ordered from
http://www.lulu.com/spotlight/unllib


Ninth printing

The front and back cover illustrations are stills from
"The Promise," an animated documentary based on
the story of Leon Malmed, produced by the Advanced
Animation Class at the College of the Canyons, Santa
Clarita, California. Image credit goes to one of the
students, Rachel Crane. The film was created with
support of Chancellor Dr. Dianne Van Hook and the
College Foundation Board under the mentorship of Ruah
Edelstein and Masha Vasilkovsky.

https://vimeo.com/236617904   [code: rcp]

# Acknowledgments

My gratitude goes to all those, too many to mention, who have entrusted me with their memories, sometimes painful. They have helped me unravel the tangled threads of the first seventy years of my life and allowing me to reconstruct the distant events more accurately.

To Pascale Martin, Jeanette Reed, Ellaraine Lockie, Bob Cliff, Ann Koch, and Maria Guerra, who each by their own perception of the events have generously extended their time and talent for the betterment of this book.

To Salomon Malmed for his contribution to this book and in memory of the difficult years we endured together.

To Catherine Ribouleau and Daniel Ribouleau, grandchildren of Henri and Suzanne Ribouleau for their moral support and lasting love.

To my sister, Rachel who inspired me to write this testimony and for her important contribution to this book with her memories.

To my brother-in-law, Izzy Epstein, to whom I am forever indebted. His generosity and persistence allowed me to rejoin my sister after a fourteen-year separation and provided me with the opportunity to flourish in America.

My affectionate thoughts go to my cousin Jacques Malmed and Aunt Sarah Blum, both now deceased, and to my cousin Jean Gerbaez with whom I still exchange jokes across the ocean. The three of them were the only family members who were born in Poland, and who immigrated to France, and survived the Holocaust.

And to my wife Patricia, whose unending support, love and steadfast encouragement during the five years it took to write this book first in French and then in English.

I am infinitely thankful to all.

This book is a tribute to Henri and Suzanne Ribouleau,
my loving second parents, Righteous among the Nations,
and to their sons René and Marcel who
by their courage and devotion saved
my life and my sister's life.


We shall forever keep their memories alive
and those of my father and mother, Srul and Chana,
the twenty members of my family, uncles,
aunts and cousins and the six million Jews
and non-Jews who were massacred
according to the diabolical plan
of the Nazis' "Final Solution."


**"They did not know it was impossible, so, they did it!"**

# Forewords

The rapid conquest of France in the early days of World War II did not prepare that country's Jewish population for what was to come. Who among them could imagine a Drancy (the primary transit camp in France for Jews being deported to Nazi death camps in the East), the evil intent of SS Captain Klaus Barbie ("The Butcher of Lyon") or the mind-wrenching collaboration of some members of the French police?

The letter from the author's parents, Srul and Chana Malmed, to their Christian neighbors asking them to send some clothes and household items to them in Drancy reveals the ability of humans to deny a worse possible scenario—that Drancy could lead to a worse place, namely Auschwitz and death. Reading Malmed's parents' note, one can imagine their optimistic thinking that a yellow measuring tape would allow them to better survive the harsh conditions of the transit camp, with Srul, a tailor by trade, bartering his sewing skills for food or favors from the guards. And, as in many letters sent from Jews to their family members and friends back home, there is the misplaced hope that they will return. Here we read Chana's promise to her neighbors, "I'll pay you back one day."

For most of this emotionally charged memoir, the all-too-familiar tragedy that was to befall the authors' parents is countered by the loving kindness of the family's neighbors, Suzanne and Henri Ribouleau, who did what only a small percentage of those under the Nazi grip did—risked everything to save a life.

In this case, it was two lives—that of Leon Malmed (then five years old) and his sister Rachel (nine), who stayed with the Ribouleaus ever since the French police knocked on their parents' door on the sunny morning of July 19, 1942 and arrested them.

Malmed grippingly brings the reader into the maelstrom of World War II Vichy France and the chaotic life of the Ribouleau parents, their two own children and their adopted charges. Most importantly, this beautifully written account captures what it was like to be a young child whose parents had disappeared and who was forced to hide his Jewish identity.

*We survived ... At last I speak* reveals the apathy of the majority in France who acquiesced to the Nazi barbarity, the acts of defiance of a few, and the remarkable courage of the Ribouleaus who swore to Monsieur and Madame Malmed that they would take care of their children until they returned. As both Papa Henri and Maman Suzanne, as Leon called them, would always respond: "These children are not hurting anyone. They need us. We will protect them."

Riva Gambert
Director, Holocaust Remembrance
Jewish Federation of the East Bay

*We survived ... At last I speak,* the story of Leon and his sister Rachel is an inspiration to everyone. It demonstrates that even within the horrors of the Holocaust there were people whose hearts were filled with kindness and courage. "Righteous Gentiles" who hid Jews risked their own lives to save others, and their acts of goodness should never be forgotten.

In these days as Holocaust Survivors are getting older and dying it is important that their stories be preserved for future generations. Leon Malmed has done a service to us all by writing his memoir.

Please share this amazing story with your children and grandchildren. We leave them with the responsibility to insure that we never forget these atrocities and that they never again happen to Jews or any other people.

Joanne Caras
Creator of *The Holocaust Survivor Cookbook* and
  *Miracles & Meals,* star of the JLTV series *Miracles
  & Meal with Joanne Caras*

Leon Malmed was born in France. He didn't come easily to writing his memoir. He was in his late 60s when he wrote it in French, and now in his 70s when he wrote the English version. It was a story he wanted to forget: the story of a 5-year old child and his 9-year old sister, whose Jewish parents were taken away by the French police under orders of the Nazis in 1942. His mother and father, desperate, were told by their neighbors "Do not worry; we will take care of your children until you come back." In a way it was a story he didn't want to remember, but finally, one he needed to tell, for both himself and the world.

To these children, who were effectively adopted by the neighbors, the truth didn't come easily, and until now the story hasn't really been told. The Ribouleaus became their parents and risked their own lives and the lives of their two sons. It is an inspiring story of turmoil and bravery by the Ribouleau family and the townspeople. It is about children who had to recognize finally that they would never see their parents again. And it is also the story about the lives of the French under the Nazi regime in France.

Leon ultimately became a successful businessman, starting his career in France and then coming to the United States. In the end it is a story of personal success, but its roots could not remain silent. It is an emotional story that brings tears both of sorrow and of heartfelt gratitude for some of the people who helped their lives. It is a story that needs to be told today as the world becomes more tribal and hate becomes more apparent. This is a book I would recommend that we all read, and then think deeply about what happened.

Bob Cliff, Ph.D.
Formerly Professor at University of California,
Berkeley, & founder of Cliff Consulting

I'm shocked, happy, and embarrassed. Shocked to be reminded that such events as described could and did take place, and shocked that it took 60 plus years to get the courage to "tell the story." Happy that a friend can finally come to terms with his own feelings and share them for family, friends, and the world, and happy to know that there are persons capable of reaching out to help in spite of personal risks and sacrifices, as demonstrated by the thousands of "Righteous" and the uncounted others. Embarrassed to have a friend open himself to such an extent, to bare such personal feelings, such personal anguish, to bare his very soul, and I'm embarrassed to be part of a human race that could inflict such pain and suffering, one human on another.

I watched World War II as a teenager from the safety of the United States. I've read the stories and accounts, seen the pictures, and visited the museums. But reading about the Holocaust from the perspective of journalists and historians is one thing. Hearing from one who actually experienced it is quite another thing entirely. Especially from one who opens himself up so totally and without reservation. The world MUST know and NOT forget. Leon Malmed's *We Survived ... At Last I Speak* is a must read.

> James W. Duke, Ed.D.
> President Emeritus, Lake Tahoe Community
> College

As observers of history, we try to comprehend World War II and its surrounding events through reading chronological accounts, watching documentaries and fictional movies and visiting Holocaust museums and concentration camps. But we are looking through a veil of distance, which keeps personal involvement safely in an intellectual place. It is personal accounts from Holocaust survivors, rather than others' interpretations, that close the distance and allow us emotional understanding, not only of the unspeakable atrocities, but of the bravery and resilience of its victims and heroes.

Leon Malmed's memoir does all this and more. A must read. *Why* you ask? The answer is because we must not become so far removed that the Holocaust is forgotten or perceived as untrue and therefore subject to repetition.

> Ellaraine Lockie
> nonfiction author/poet/essayist /educator

I am the granddaughter my grandparents, who perished in Auschwitz, never got to meet.

For the Jewish people then, the Nazi nightmare was incomprehensible. For all people now, the torturing and murdering of 12 million people—six million of them Jewish—seems hard to believe.

My mother, Rachel Malmed Epstein, and uncle, Leon Malmed, are witnesses to what we've been reading about for the last 70 years. They are two of the lucky few who escaped death at the hands of the Nazis thanks to the courage and decency of those few who dared to be defiant.

The focus and message of this amazing story is that of true heroism and goodness. What goodness could possibly come from such a horrific era in history?

As bleak a period as the Holocaust was, it provided the stage for many heroes and heroines—non-Jewish people who did what they did because they were decent and made split-second decisions without giving thought to their own fate.

Henri and Suzanne Ribouleau, a French Catholic couple, took in two young Jewish children at a time when Jews were considered the plague. They risked not only their lives, but the lives of their two teen-aged sons as well. The Ribouleaus never seemed to grasp the heroism and magnitude of their actions during the war.

Truly righteous people in every sense of the word.

Rachel's and her brother Leon's survival is one big miracle.

The story of survival continues way beyond the end of the war and the paths each sibling's life took—both ending in the United States of America.

Thank you, Uncle Leon, for writing this book. It is a true treasure.

Anita Epstein Leibowitz
Assistant Professor, Communications
Suffolk County Community College
Long Island, New York

*I dedicate this book to Henri and Suzanne Ribouleau*
*and their two sons René and Marcel.*
*Without their courage, my life would have ended at the age of seven.*


*My thoughts go to my wife Patricia,*
*my children Olivier, Corinne, and James*
*and my grandchildren Rayce, Jake, and Rhyder.*

# Contents

Chapter 1

# July 19, 1942

It is a summer day.

My father wakes up at dawn. Like every Sunday, he gets himself ready without making any noise so as not to wake us up. He is waiting for Marcel Ribouleau, our neighbor's son, who accompanies him on his expeditions throughout the countryside. Times are hard. Food is scarce, so Papa exchanges clothes for poultry, butter, eggs, fruit and vegetables.

At 5:30 a.m. someone knocks at the door.

My father opens. At the doorway, much to his surprise, are two French police officers, "gendarmes," he knows very well. He has often done favors for them, repairing worn-out uniforms at no charge, as he is a tailor by profession. But they have never come so early in the morning, on a Sunday, no less.

The two policemen seem embarrassed. One of them clears his throat. The second man gazes downward.

"Mr Malmed," one finally says, "you must accompany us immediately to the police station. He emphasizes the word "immediately".

"But why?" asks my father, surprised.

They don't offer an explanation.

Awakened by the discussion, my mother comes out onto the landing. She has hurriedly thrown on a robe over her nightgown, which she has buttoned up crookedly.

"Your husband must follow us," repeats one of the policemen, decisively.

"But why? What's going on?" she asks.

"Let's not waste time," one policeman replies, raising his voice.

"I'll come with you," my mother adds. "It must be a mistake."

Looking pale, she clenches her fists. She suddenly thinks of us. "But what about our children?" She is nearly crying.

I am four-and-a-half years old, and my sister Rachel will soon be ten. The loud voices have woken my sister and me. I don't want

1

to stay alone in the bedroom. Clutching my sister's hand, we join our parents. As soon as our mother sees us she cannot hold her tears back any longer. Frightened by the gendarmes and seeing my mother crying, I run to her, also in tears and grab onto her robe.

"Why?" she repeats.

Papa asks again "What have we done?"

Neither understands what is wanted from them, they are frightened and the questions remain unanswered.

The policemen are growing impatient. The tone of their voices becomes hard. "Don't make such a fuss," one says. "Hurry up, get dressed and follow us!"

We live in a very quiet neighborhood. Such noise is even more unusual because it is so early on a Sunday morning. Our neighbors are awakened by the loud voices. Mr Ribouleau, our neighbor, who lives in the apartment below us, climbs three stairs at a time. It is so early that he is still wearing his pajamas.

"What is happening, monsieur Malmed?" he asks.

Searching for his words, my father explains that the policemen have come to arrest him. They will not say why.

"They must have made a mistake. Don't worry," says Mr Ribouleau. He is a calm, even-keeled man in his thirties.

"You will be back in an hour," he adds confidently.

"Yes, yes," replies my mother in a choked voice. "Rachel, take care of Léon. I will be back soon."

My mother tries hard to hold back her tears; she does not want us to worry. My parents return to their bedroom to get dressed. One policeman follows them. He demands that the bedroom door be left open. The one on the landing looks at his watch impatiently.

A few minutes later, my parents come out looking desperate as the gendarmes grumble "Hurry up!" I try to run to my mother, but monsieur Ribouleau holds my hand firmly.

"They will be back in less than an hour," Mr Ribouleau repeats assuredly.

Stunned and frightened, we watch them go away. I hurry with Rachel to the window of the living room overlooking the street. Mr Ribouleau puts his arm around our shoulders. The three of us wait silently, our foreheads glued to the glass.

About an hour and a half later, we see them coming down the street with a gendarme on each side.

"Maman! Papa!" we scream.

"You see, it was a mistake," begins Mr Ribouleau, with a hearty smile that brightens up his welcoming face.

Suddenly, he is quiet. Maman looks extremely distraught. Her eyes are swollen with tears. My father is disheveled.

"They have a warrant to arrest both of us," he says. "They wouldn't tell us why. We have come back to pick up some personal belongings." My father's voice is shaky. He tries very hard not to break down.

Why didn't the policemen immediately tell my mother that she was also to be arrested? They had to know that my parents were arrested for the simple reason that they were Jewish. They obeyed blindly the orders of the SS.

It is also possible they were too embarrassed. They had known my parents for a number of years and undoubtedly appreciated my father's kindness and generosity. Why didn't they forewarn my parents the evening before, or even during the night?

My parents had returned on foot from the police station to our home, 17 rue Saint Fiacre. We lived on the top floor of the three-story apartment building. We had moved here a year after we came back to Compiègne from Paris when the German bombings in 1940 had destroyed our home on "rue du Donjon."

We are all scared. What will our parents do with us?

Who is going to take care of us?

To whom will they hand us over?

How long will they be away?

Why have they been arrested?

They have not committed any crime or infraction to justify their arrest. So many questions without any answers!

Mr Clausse, our first floor neighbor, advised my father a number of times to go into hiding. He didn't listen to him.

Our parents believed that the Germans were arresting only rich Jews. They were not wealthy so they did not worry. Besides, where would they have gone?

They probably wondered who else was arrested that day. So many thoughts must have been racing through their minds during that short journey back to the apartment.

"They're arresting foreign Jews," our father tells us. "Why? For how long?" someone asks. "We don't know," my father answers in a tired voice.

It is probably the first time that we see my parents cry. Everyone is crying except for the gendarmes.

My mother asks Rachel to run to our Jewish friends who live close by.

"Tell them to come and take both of you to their home."

My sister leaves quickly. She rings the doorbell several times. She knocks on the door. She calls out. No one answers. She races back home.

"There is no one there," she says out of breath.

My parents are on the verge of collapse, panic-stricken.

"What are we going to do? What will happen to our children?" my mother asks.

"Hurry up. Hurry up," repeat the policemen, now irritated. They are totally indifferent to the terror we all feel.

"Mr and Mrs Malmed don't worry. My wife and I will take care of your children until you return," says Mr Ribouleau, a good neighbor, not even a friend.

This simple sentence saved my life and that of my sister. It changed the course of our existence and the future of our families.

He spoke soothingly. His wife had joined us after hearing the commotion. She takes my mother's hands to reassure her, and says:

"Don't worry, Mrs Malmed. Your children will be fine when you return."

In tears, my parents go back to their bedroom and pack a suitcase. One of the "gendarmes," stands in the doorway, watching them.

"Come on, hurry up!" he says.

My mother piles some clothes into a suitcase. Tears roll down her cheeks. Rachel and I cry and moan—we are scared to death!

Mr Clausse's wife, a young, discrete and unassuming neighbor, hears the noise and comes to see what is happening.

"The police officers have arrested them. They are taking them away," whispers Madame Ribouleau.

"But how is that possible? And what about the children?" Madame Clausse asks, almost shouts.

"Let's go, let's go," urges one of the gendarmes.

"What a time we live in! My God! How can such things happen?" exclaims Mrs Clausse.

The gendarmes are impatient and urging my parents to leave the apartment.

My father hands a bottle of wine he had kept for a "special occasion" to Mr Ribouleau.

"We'll drink it together at the end of the war," he says and adds as quietly as possible, "The tires ... money ... in the garage."

My parents rented a garage where they kept their car and their merchandise. It was common at that time not to leave cars in the street to avoid exposure to bad weather and theft. They had also hidden some money there in case their apartment was burglarized.

The gendarmes are urging my parents towards the stairs. I latch onto them. Rachel screams: "Maman! Papa!"

"My children! My children!" pleads my mother.

The policemen push us back and my parents are forced down the stairs struggling with their suitcase. Mrs Ribouleau holds us close to her. From the window in the living room, we watch them walking away with four policemen this time, two others were standing at the door to our building. My father is pulling his hair out and is shouting. My mother turns her head to catch sight of us. Tears stream down her face.

"I will try to get some information," says Mr Ribouleau, still believing a mistake has been made.

He follows them from a safe distance on his bike all the way to the police station located a couple of miles away. There, we were told years later, my parents were immediately handed over to the German SS. Mr Ribouleau tries in vain to question the gendarmes as to their destination but gets no answer.

The next day, Mr Ribouleau went to the garage my father had mentioned. The doors had been forced open and the tires and money had disappeared. Were the "gendarmes" involved? We'll never know, not that it matters.

This is how Maman and Papa brutally and suddenly disappeared from our lives. We did not know when we would see them again. We never thought at that moment it could be never.

Of this day, I only remember my sister and I crying and screaming while hanging onto our mother's dress. I was four and a half years old, my sister, ten. She remembers.

It was July 19, 1942, a despicable day.

Chapter 2

# A Lost World

My parents were born in Brest-on-the-Bug, a village close to Brest-Litovsk, located in what was formerly eastern Poland. Today, Brest-Litovsk, re-named Brest, is part of Belarus with a population of about 300,000. I know little about their youth. Like most Jews in that region, my parents grew up in a ghetto. The Malmed and Blum families were neighbors. As children, they played daily with each other.

My paternal grandmother was called "Boubé," the Yiddish word for grandmother. Her name was Rivka Malmed. She was born in 1880 in Brest-Litovsk. Szyja Malmed, my grandfather, died of typhus in his mid-thirties. My grandmother was thirty years old at the time, and they already had eight children. My father, Srul, born on May 13, 1906 was the third oldest among the six boys and the two girls.

As a widow, Boubé baked bread to earn money to buy food. All the children helped with the bakery. Some of them were too small to reach the tabletop. They stood on bricks to knead the dough. For the most part, the work was done at night since Jews were not allowed by law to own a business. Boubé made sure—I don't know how—that the oven chimney did not smoke excessively to avoid attracting the attention of the authorities. Life was very difficult for Jewish people. The underground bakery was often visited by the authorities and arbitrarily closed. Because her bread was good and the community depended on it, the Christian population would immediately ask the local authorities to reopen the bakery, which they did most of the time.

The children delivered the bread each morning to both Jewish and non-Jewish families. Cossacks* also came regularly to get their

---

* Cossacks: members of a people noted for their horsemanship and employed for military duties.

6

*My parents Chana and Srul Malmed, 1936*

bread, but most of them refused to pay. They claimed that Jews should not own a business and certainly not become wealthy at the expense of Christian people.

Winters were bitterly cold. The family, when the baking was done, slept in the basement close to the oven, which was always on. The Blum children stayed with them too, as they could not afford to keep the fire going all night in their home. Both families were very poor.

Their homemade wooden-soled shoes, tied to their feet with leather straps, hardly provided any protection from the snow and the cold. My Aunt Sarah Blum once told me a frightening story that took place one winter. One morning, she and my father were walking across the frozen river Bug, to deliver bread on the other side of the river. Suddenly, twelve-year-old Sarah broke through the ice. My father grabbed her by her hair and managed to pull her out of the icy water. Life was hard and precarious in those days.

Jews have lived in Poland since the twelfth century. Prior to World War II, there were three million Jews in the country, about ten percent of the population. Today, there are less than 20,000. 2.9 million were exterminated during the war. Despite the fact that they were living in Poland for close to eight hundred years, they were forced to live apart from the Christian population. The authorities made it difficult for them to get an education. Jews had to pay exorbitant fees to attend college.

For centuries religious teachings had spread lies about Jewish people, contributing to strong anti-Semitic feelings. Among other things, Jews were accused of killing Christ and of using human blood to make the traditional matzos for Passover. Yet, interestingly, Jews were allowed to vote. During election campaigns, persecution and harassment were put on hold. Candidates, promising major improvements, campaigned in Jewish neighborhoods. Cossacks, always on horseback, were more tolerant in the pre-electoral times. Usually, they took pleasure in hitting people with their whips as they galloped by. As soon as the campaign was over, conditions returned to the pre-election state with no improvements whatsoever.

I can only imagine the hopelessness and the laborious lives of my father and his brothers and sisters, Zelman, Ida, Meyer, Joseph, Sarah, Eizik, Nathan, and their mother Rivka. There are no remaining survivors of that time. My Aunt Sarah Blum, the last one of that era, passed away in 2002.

Today, these ghosts of an almost forgotten time of history are just faces on the few photos, yellowed by time, that survived the World War II disaster. In a picture taken in 1928, my father is sitting in a Polish uniform, unsmiling. In another photo he is with handsome and smartly dressed friends. Two of them wear an elegant hat, one a boater, tilted to one side.

It seems that in those days people did not smile when they had their picture taken. Jews especially had little reason to. Children, too, stood like statues, seemingly petrified. Looking at them now, the photographs reflect the dark times in which they lived and the foreboding of the horrors that lay ahead. Each photo reflects a black-and-white world of grave-looking people, alive but already brushing death.

I have never been to Brest-Litovsk. Most likely I would find no trace of my uncles, aunts, cousins, parents, grandparents, and great grandparents. As far as I know, the government of Belarus has never expressed a desire to redress the wrongs that were done to its Jewish citizens.

My mother, Chana Blum, was born in 1911. The exact date is un-

*Charles (Calel) Blum (my mother's brother), a friend, Meyer Malmed
(my father's brother), Srul Malmed (my father), 1931*

known. She lost both her parents when she was nine years old during a typhus epidemic. She had five brothers and two sisters. Her older brother Calel (Charles) managed to take care of his siblings. After emigrating to France, my Uncle Calel married Sarah Malmed, my father's younger sister.

Uncle Zelman, the eldest son of the Malmed family, emigrated to France in 1923. He settled in Saint-Quentin, a town located about one hundred miles north of Paris. There, he worked as a tailor in a clothing store. Before leaving Poland he married Sarah Blum, my mother's sister who was born July 13, 1900. The couple had three children, Jacques, Ida, and Sonia Malmed. A tragic end awaited two of them.

Life became increasingly difficult for Jews in Poland. Food was scarce. There was "not a single piece of meat in the pot," Aunt Sarah Blum remembered. In their quest to escape poverty, persecu-

Left to right: *Sarah Malmed, my aunt; Chana Blum, my mother;
"Boubé", my grandmother; Meyer Malmed, Salomon's father, my
uncle; Jean Gerbaëz, son of Ida, my cousin; Abraham Gerbaëz, Ida's
husband, my uncle; Ida Malmed, wife of Abraham Gerbaez,
my aunt; Hélène Gerbaëz, daughter of Abraham and
Ida, a cousin, and Srul Malmed, my father, 1928.*

tion, and famine, Charles Blum, my mother's brother, emigrated to
France in 1929.

A year later, Srul along with his sister Sarah and their mother,
Rivka, emigrated to France as well. Zelman, my uncle, helped them
financially. They arrived in Saint-Quentin after a long, tiring trip.
Completely lost and penniless, they ended up in Paris at the "Gare
du Nord" train station, one hundred miles past their intended stop
in Saint-Quentin. A generous woman felt sorry for these strangers
who spoke no French and had no French money. She bought them a
train ticket from Paris to Saint-Quentin. Aunt Sarah Blum recalled
that this Good Samaritan walked them to the platform where their
train was to depart and waited until the train left. Coming from Poland where the non-Jewish population hated them, it was hard to
believe that a stranger would help people who were badly dressed
and did not even speak French.

My father and mother had known each other since childhood.
They dated before emigrating to France. Both my mother and father

*Wedding of Srul Malmed and Chana Blum, 1931*

left Brest-Litovsk at about the same time. Shortly after their arrival in France, a friend of the family, Joseph Epelberg, who lived in Paris, came to Saint-Quentin to visit with the Malmed and Blum families, but mainly to court my mother. My mother was a pretty woman. My father was furious with him and practically dragged him to the train station, ordered him to leave on the next train and never come back. "Chana will be my wife!" he told him. My father and mother were madly in love. They married in Saint-Quentin in 1931. Several years later, Joseph Epelberg and his wife Suzanne became very good friends of my parents.

Aunt Blum often talked about Uncle Charles, her husband, owning only one pair of pants and two shirts for the first couple of years in France! He made a living by pulling a small trailer behind his bicycle, loaded with socks and men's underwear that he sold door-to-door.

Aunt Sarah worked for a textile company where they processed cotton. It was a sweatshop with long hours and unsanitary working conditions, which eventually burned down.

Their oldest daughter, Rachel, was born in 1932, followed by her sister, Madeleine, in 1937. Aunt Sarah quit her job in the textile plant to work with her husband at the open markets. By this time, Uncle Charles had replaced his bicycle and trailer with a small van.

Whatever the season, their day began at 5:00 a.m. to allow time to get to market and set up the stall.

For most of the Malmed and Blum families, emigrating to France was to have been temporary. One of the Blum sisters, Rose, moved to the United States in 1922 at the age of 17. It was hoped that she would bring the members of the Blum and Malmed families to America, but immigration quotas were very limited and Aunt Rose did not have the financial guarantees the government required to bring the family.

As time passed, those who had emigrated to France began to take root and adapt to this welcoming country and its lifestyle. Couples married and children were born. Everyone was learning French. New friends were made. Life was relatively easy. Few wanted to move again to another country, struggle with a new language, find a way to earn a living and essentially start all over.

Meanwhile, two Malmed brothers, Nathan and Eizik, remained in Poland. Unfortunately, they were exterminated along with the other 2.9 million Polish Jews.

In 1933 my parents moved to Compiègne to work with Uncle Zelman. Compiègne was a small town of about 18,000 people located about fifty miles north of Paris. Uncle Zelman owned a store in a modest, three-story building, close to the bridge crossing the Oise River leading to the nearby train station. Uncle Zelman and his family lived on the first floor above the store, my parents on the second floor and Uncle Joseph on the third floor.

My father worked as a tailor for his brother, and my mother as a seamstress in a clothing factory in Compiègne. Uncle Zelman wasn't an easy man to work for. He was hard on his employees, my father included. He was a chain smoker until the day he died despite the fact that he suffered from asthma and had trouble breathing. I can still remember the yellow paper he used to roll his cigarettes. It was believed then that yellow paper was not as harmful as the white paper. His difficulties breathing caused him to make strange faces, which made all of us children laugh.

A sign hung above his boutique: "The tailor of Roubaix, suits for 280 francs" (equivalent to $180). A few people in Compiègne still remember that he would give away prized gifts like small knives to customers to thank them for their loyalty. He was a very well known tailor and had many loyal customers. His business was so good that

*My parents Srul, and Chana Malmed with Rachel, 1935*

he could not find enough qualified employees in Compiègne. He sent trunks filled with material to subcontractors in Paris.

Everyone in the family spoke Yiddish at home and French outside. My parents learned French rather quickly. They were happy in France. They had run away from the misery, the pogroms and the hateful environment to a country where they could work freely, without fear, and send their children to public school without having to bribe someone.

My sister, Rachel, was born on April 29, 1932. I followed five years later on October 4, 1937.

Chapter 3

# Before the Storm

Rachel has often told me that my parents were ecstatic—especially my father—when my mother gave birth to a son, a sweet-looking baby with a lot of thick, black curly hair.

My father was convinced that I was the most handsome and probably the most intelligent boy in the world! For the last five years Rachel had received my parents' full attention. When I came along, they were so happy with having a boy and gave me so much attention that she felt she was no longer loved. On my eighth day, family and friends came to Compiègne from Paris and other towns for the circumcision ceremony.

My first four birthdays were major events. I was treated like a little prince, which made Rachel feel a bit jealous and neglected. I did not know until much later in life that I had been given such preferential treatment.

I cannot think of my early childhood without thinking of my cousin Charles. Everyone called him Charlot, the only son of Uncle Joseph and Aunt Madeleine. He was born on October 10, 1938, almost a year to the day after me. He was a handsome boy with long, black and curly hair. We probably played together, but I don't remember. When Uncle Joseph was young, he had an accident and an unsuccessful operation left him lame. He had a pronounced limp, which probably sent him to the gas chamber on his arrival in Auschwitz.

I was too young to remember any of my family, aunts and uncles from Paris or Saint-Quentin whom I had met before the war.

My cousin Salomon, two years older than I, is the son of Meyer Malmed, one of my father's brothers and Gela Kibel. Salomon's childhood was also disrupted during the Occupation. He assured me that he had never seen Rachel or me before our arrival in Saint-Quentin in September 1947.

Salomon's father died in 1937 at the age of twenty-nine from post-operative complications a week after stomach surgery. Salo-

*Léon Malmed, 1937*

mon's mother remarried two years later. She was deported to Auschwitz with her second husband, Joseph Borowicz, in 1944 and
exterminated. Salomon survived, thanks to the humanitarian organization, O.S.E., *Oeuvre de Secours aux Enfants\**, an organization
created by doctors in 1912 in Saint Petersburg, Russia to help needy
children of the Jewish population. Branches of O.S.E. were later established in other countries. They saved the lives of thousands of
Jewish children during World War II. Salomon wrote about his experience during the war in a testimony titled *Sali,†* which was his
fake identity during the war.

My parents and my Uncle Joseph were shopkeepers. My parents
sold children's clothes; Uncle Joseph sold leather and sheepskin
jackets as well as women's and men's coats. They worked the open

---

\* Organization to Save the Children
† *Sali*, by Saloman Malmed (Editions Le Manuscrit, 2005).

Left to right: *Ida Malmed, my cousin, Rachel, my sister,*
*Uncle Zelman, Boubé, my grandmother, Rachel Blum,*
*and my father Srul Malmed, 1933*

markets of Compiègne on Wednesdays and Saturdays and in the
surrounding towns the other days of the week. They made a modest
and steady living.

Nearly every morning, Papa and Maman walked fifteen minutes
to the garage in rue Vivenel to pick up their van, then dropped me
off at the nursery before driving to the town where the market was
being held that day.

Dedicated nuns ran the nursery. I still remember one of them in
particular. She greeted me each morning with a welcoming smile.
Her large headdress was so white and stiff that I thought it was
made out of cardboard! Plastics did not exist in those days. I wondered if she had any hair, for none could be seen.

My sister Rachel went to the public school, "Jeanne d'Arc," one
block away from our home. The discipline was very strict. Rachel,
who was unruly at times, was terrified when she was sent to the
principal's office.

My parents returned from the markets around 2:00 p.m. They

*Suzanne holding Fanny Epelberg, Chana, my mother, and Léon, 1938*

picked me up at the nursery before going home. After lunch, they walked down to Uncle Zelman's workshop behind the store where they manufactured garments.

Along with my father and my Uncle Joseph, there were two young apprentices in the shop.

Uncle Zelman had a driver's license, but he hated to drive. Mr Patte, owner of the bakery a few doors away, drove Uncle Zelman around. Mr Patte suffered from respiratory problems as a result of having been gassed during WWI. As a veteran, he hated wars with a passion. He was a kind person and a very good friend of the family.

Every year, Uncle Zelman took his wife and three children to Mont Dore, a spa town located near Clermont Ferrand in the center of France. Uncle Joseph, his wife Madeleine, and their son Charles always joined them.

In the summer, my mother and her sister Sarah Blum, Ida, Zelman's wife, Madeleine Malmed, Joseph's wife, and sometimes Suzanne Epelberg, her friend from Paris, would walk to the park of the Castle in Compiègne close to the center of town.

*My mother with Leon, 1937*

The women knitted, sitting on a bench or on the grass, while Fanny and I played on the beautifully manicured green lawns surrounded by magnificent flowerbeds.

What did they talk about? What were they dreaming of? They probably spoke about their children's future and about a nice home they would own one day. I would love to know. Maybe they were imagining the kings, queens and other royalty strolling in these very same royal gardens a few centuries before.

On Sundays, when the weather allowed and they had no urgent work, my parents would prepare a picnic. We would spend the afternoon on the banks of the Oise river or in the park Songeon a few blocks away. Almost every evening during the week, after work and while my mother prepared dinner, my father took a walk with my sister and me. He carried me on his shoulders to the corner of our street and the town main street, rue Solférino. We watched the pedestrians, bicyclists and the few cars. Papa was excited by the cars.

"Look," he would say, "a Renault or a Chenard and Walker! What a magnificent car! One day, we'll have one just like that!"

We could hear the trains at the station close by, on the other side of the bridge. My father would imitate the sound of the train's whistle to make us laugh.

Little did he know that soon he and my mother would leave from a train station some thirty miles away, shoved by rifle butts into a cattle car, standing with a hundred other innocent people for four or five days toward a tragic destiny.

I have only a few photos of these happy years along with hazy bits of memories. My sister Rachel and my cousins Jacques Malmed and Jean Gerbaez have helped me recall.

According to testimonies from our neighbors and friends, my parents were kind and generous people. They made a very handsome couple. They loved each other; they kissed often (which was, I was told, rare among Eastern Europeans); no one had ever heard them quarrel. Discrete and unassuming, my parents devoted themselves to their children and their work. I was told that my mother's voice was always calm and soft-spoken. Maman's voice ... I seem to hear it when I think about it, although I know it's only a mirage brought on by nostalgia and desire.

My cousin Jacques remembered the rumors of the pre-war years. Concentration camps in Germany were talked about but nothing was said about extermination camps. Who could ever imagine that such an abomination was possible, yet German architects, engineers and manufacturers were diligently working on designing and manufacturing the industrial human death factories.

The peaceful lives of many were about to be toppled. The upheaval of war was about to inflict deep wounds that would "never" heal.

Chapter 4

# The Downfall

In March 1939, Hitler moved into the remainder of Czechoslovakia, whose annexation had started in 1938. On September 1, 1939, Germany invaded Poland; Great Britain and France declared war with Germany on September 3, 1939. The "Normal Life" and happiness of millions was suddenly shattered.

A contingent of volunteer Polish men residing in France was rapidly put together and placed under French military authority. My father and Uncle Charles Blum enlisted immediately.

Poland was overrun by October 6, 1939; the "Phony War"* of 1939–1940 lasted several months. There were major changes in our lives with the absence of our father. From the front lines he wrote to us with always positive news. The calm ended on May 19, 1940, when Germany began bombing northern France.

France had—naïvely and at great expense—built the "Maginot Line" on its border with Germany to discourage an invasion. It was a fortified line of defense built to be impassable. However, the Maginot Line proved ineffective, as German troops did not invade France at the Franco-German border. Instead, they swept through Holland and Luxembourg into Belgium, a neutral country. Belgium, certain that its neutrality would be respected, had refused to let the British Expeditionary Forces or the French troops be stationed there, a move that might have stopped the German invasion, or at least delayed it. The German army encountered very little resistance, and within a short time, they crossed the Belgium-French border where France had no defenses in place. This

---

* The "Phony War," from October 1939 to the Battle of France in May 1940, was marked by the lack of major military operations by the Western Allies against the German Reich. The terms of the Anglo-Polish and Franco-Polish military alliances had forced the United Kingdom and France to assist Poland, but they were not prepared for war.

fatal error was made in an effort to avoid offending Belgium, its neighbor.

France surrendered three weeks after the start of the hostilities. During those three weeks, the panic-stricken people living in northern France went on a chaotic exodus south, fleeing the advancing German army which fired indiscriminately at soldiers and civilians.

On a single day, May 17, sixty-four people, both residents and fleeing refugees, died in Compiègne as a result of German air strikes. The center of our town was destroyed by three days of German bombing and artillery fire. Our apartment building—close to the two strategic targets: the train station and the bridge over the river Oise, connecting the main road from North to South—was in ruins. We had nothing left except the van with the merchandise fortunately parked in the garage, one mile away, which was spared from destruction. We all rushed out as soon as the siren called the alert and ran for the nearest underground shelter. Miraculously, no one in our family was hurt. When we came out of the shelter, our building was still collapsing. Horrified, my mother burst into tears as she held us tightly, our cousin Jacques told us.

What would become of her, alone with two children and no income?

We had been without news of my father for a few weeks. He was on the front line. We did not know where he was. We could only guess that he was in a German prison camp, or worse, dead.

The exodus intensified. The Baroness of Rothschild, whose husband was the mayor of Compiègne, arranged the evacuation of the residents by bringing public buses from Paris. Very few people had cars in those days, unless they used one for work. My mother didn't have a driver's license and she had never driven a car. Nevertheless, she decided to get the van parked in the garage we rented on "rue Vivenel." She was able to get the car started, maybe with some help, I was too young to remember, and headed for Paris with my sister and me. The roads were crowded with thousands of refugees in cars, on bicycles and on foot. Destroyed cars, trucks and carriages with their horses dead but still attached, were scattered along on the road creating huge gridlocks. Uncle Zelman and Uncle Joseph were also fleeing with their families. Once in Paris, we settled into a hotel in rue d'Hauteville, that our friends, the Epelberg family, had reserved for us.

On June 9, 1940, the German troops occupied Compiègne, our hometown. The few people remaining in town stayed in their basements for a few days.

Holland, Belgium and Luxembourg had surrendered to Germany. Paris was occupied on June 14, 1940. Paul Reynaud, Prime Minister of France, refusing to be party to a peace agreement with Germany, resigned on June 16. Philippe Pétain, recently named Minister of State, became the leader of the government. On June 17, Pétain delivered a broadcast to the French people announcing that he had asked the Germans for an armistice. On June 22, France signed an armistice with Germany that gave Germany control over the north and west of the country, including Paris and the Atlantic coastline.

Adolf Hitler deliberately chose Compiègne as the place to sign the World War II armistice, due to its symbolic role in history. It was the site where Maréchal Foch and the German plenipotentiaries met on November 11, 1918, in a railroad car to sign the World War I armistice with a defeated Germany.

Before Hitler came to Compiègne, to satisfy his thirst for revenge, he ordered his troops to burn down the remaining standing structures in the center of town. Flame-throwers were used, and more than six hundred buildings were destroyed.

On the afternoon of June 21, 1940, Hitler was flown over the ravaged town, rejoicing at the punishment inflicted. He landed at 2:30 p.m. at the Margny-les-Compiègne airfield, a few miles away from Compiègne. He must have gloated over the destruction he wreaked to avenge the humiliation of Germany's defeat in 1918. The roads across town were cleared for the Nazi leader. The monster rode in a large, black Mercedes through Compiègne, now in ruins, to the "Carrefour de l'Armistice" in Rethondes, on the outskirts of Compiègne.

He stopped to read the inscription engraved on an enormous granite block, twenty-four by eighteen feet, recalling the Allied and American victory:

> *Here on November 11, 1918, succumbed the criminal*
> *pride of the German Empire vanquished by the free*
> *people which it intended to enslave.*

*Inscription on the stone in the middle of the "Clairière de l'Armistice"*

Hitler climbed into the historical railroad car and sat in the same chair in which Marshal Ferdinand Foch* had sat when he faced the defeated German representatives.

After listening to the reading of the preamble, Hitler, in a calculated gesture of disdain to the French delegates, left the railroad car. Goering, Hess, Ribbentropp and members of top German military management led by General Keitel accompanied him.

The Second World War Armistice between Nazi Germany and France was signed the next day, on June 22.

Hitler ordered all the monuments in the clearing destroyed except the statue of Marshal Foch, the railroad car, and the granite Memorial. The railroad car as well as the dismantled granite Memorial were sent to Berlin. Hitler ordered the statue of Marshall Foch to be left intact so that it would be honoring only a wasteland. The Alsace-Lorraine Monument depicting a German eagle impaled by a sword was destroyed and all evidence of the site was obliterated. The railway car itself was moved from Berlin to Crawinkel in Thuringia,

---

* Marshal Foch (1851–1929) was French commander of Allied forces in World War I.

*Location of the railroad car in which the WWI armistice was signed*

Germany. In 1945 Hitler ordered it destroyed by SS troops and the remains buried.

Hitler and his entourage returned to Germany after stopping briefly at staff headquarters in the Sessevalle-Soultrait mansion, the former residence of Pétain.

The World was changed forever. Under unimaginable conditions, tens of millions of innocent men, women and children would perish over the next four years.

Miraculously, the bridge over the river "Oise" leading to the railroad station had been spared. When the Germans occupied our town on June 9, 1940, very few people had remained; most had fled south as soon as the German armies crossed the French-Belgian border. Compiègne was burning. Fire Chief Captain Fournaise and his firefighters fought the fires the whole week of June 28, 1940.

France had capitulated. France was occupied. The armistice was expected to end the miseries of the war, but it turned out to be the beginning of a reign of terror.

Slowly, people began returning to their hometowns. James de Rothschild, the mayor of Compiègne, a Jew, had joined the Allied

Forces in London. His second in command, deputy mayor, Paul Co-syns, assumed the mayor's responsibilities.

A lot needed to be done. The enemy confiscated food, cars, homes, gas and oil, and took over all manufacturing complexes. People struggled to find the most basic supplies. Bakeries needed flour, butchers needed to drive to farms but had no means of trans-portation, the sick needed medical attention, senior citizens whose houses were demolished needed to be relocated, streets needed to be cleared of destroyed cars and trucks. Animal corpses needed to be disposed of. Empty houses needed to be requisitioned for the homeless, and temporary barracks needed to be built for storeown-ers and craftsmen who had lost their shops.

Shortly after the armistice was signed, our father was demobi-lized. To avoid being captured, he had dressed in civilian clothes before the German army got to his unit. If he had been taken pris-oner, he probably would have been saved from deportation.

Papa appeared suddenly at our apartment in Paris, exhausted and dirty, Rachel recalls. He was so happy to see us again and be with us. Joseph Epelberg remembered seeing me jump into my fa-ther's arms and not wanting to let go.

"The war is over!" Papa was repeating, embracing the three of us.

"Everything will get back to normal again," he was saying cheer-fully, full of hope.

"But what will the Germans do? What will happen to us, Jews? What about the rumors we hear increasingly?" my mother was asking.

"Oh, they have got more important things to worry about in-stead of us!" my father told her.

We remained in Paris for a few more months.

My Uncle Charles Blum was captured by the Germans still wear-ing his army uniform and was taken prisoner. To avoid detection of his jewishness, he had discarded his identity papers and ver-bally added an "i" to his surname. To the Germans, he was known as "Charles Blumi," which sounded French. He was kept prisoner of war for five years in Köln, Germany, at the "Stalag 12D". Upon his ar-rival at the camp, he declared himself a cabinetmaker, a trade that he had never practiced, but one that he liked and hoped that such a specialty would keep him away from hard labor. He was sent to a lo-cal shop owned by Herr Shumaker. This man, I suspect, appreciated having an employee that he didn't have to pay, even if this extra hand was only able to do janitorial work to start with. To hide his accent and not give away his foreign background, Uncle Charles spoke as little as possible. The Germans never found out that he was Jewish. All prisoners had to shower twice a week, which presented a dangerous situation for him. He always faced the wall so that no one would see that he was circumcised. In those days, only Jews were circumcised. Somehow, he survived the war.

In 1941, we returned to Compiègne along with our Uncle Joseph, his wife Madeleine, and their son, my cousin Charlot. Uncle Zelman and the rest of the family decided to remain in Paris. There were heated discussions about whether to stay in Paris or return to Compiègne. The future revealed that this decision would not matter.

"I have no confidence in the Nazis,"* repeated Zelman. "They're capable of anything. Paris is a large city. We can hide more easily here if they ever invade France."

"But getting food supplies will be easier in Compiègne," argued my father. "I know so many people there. The children will be better off in the countryside. War will go on elsewhere. What can the Germans do to us? To them, we don't exist. We are subhumans."

Finally, our families separated in anguish as we left Paris. Who could have imagined that day that most of them would never see each other again?

Sadly Uncle Zelman, who had felt that Paris was safer, saw his wife and two daughters arrested during the July 16 and 17, 1942 infamous roundup raid, Rafle du Vel' d'Hiv code-named by the French Pétain government "Operation Spring Breeze". My aunt and two cousins either died during the transport or on their arrival at the extermination camp.

When we returned to Compiègne the local French administration provided us with an apartment where we stayed for nearly a year. When the owners came back and claimed their property, we moved to "17, rue Saint Fiacre."

---

* The Nazi Party was born out of the German Workers Party in the 1920s. Led by Adolf Hitler, it took control of Germany in 1933.

# Chapter 5

# 17 rue Saint Fiacre

Rue Saint Fiacre, Compiègne, where we lived, is a small street about two hundred yards long. It is located between rue de Paris and rue St. Germain. At that time, rue de Paris was the most direct route from Paris to Belgium and used by all military convoys.

"17 rue Saint Fiacre" is a three-story brick building half way down the street with three identical apartments. The bottom half of the door to the street was a light-colored wood; the upper half an opaque glass protected by black forged ornamental-iron bars. The wood and glass door opens into a narrow hallway that leads to the first floor apartment, to the staircase and the second and third floor apartments, and to the backyard and the garden. From the hallway there is another staircase going down to the basement laundry room and the three cellars.

We lived on the third floor. Upon entering our apartment, there was a hallway that opened to the kitchen, the toilet, the dining room, my parent's bedroom, and my sister's small bedroom. That room had barely enough space for two children's beds and a cupboard. My crib was next to my parent's bed. The only source of heating for the entire apartment came from the kitchen wood-burning stove. The kitchen was my playground. My toys were the pieces of wood used to keep the stove going. I spent most days in that room.

We lived very simply. My parents bought second-hand furniture at auctions. The dining/living room was completely empty except for a large worktable and two sewing machines my parents used to alter clothes and sew new ones that they sold at the open markets. On Sundays, my father exchanged clothes or sewing services for food with farmers in the countryside. He pulled a two-wheel trailer full of merchandise behind his bicycle ten to twenty miles every Sunday.

Marcel and Rolande Clausse, our first-floor neighbors, had three daughters. The Ribouleau family Henri, Suzanne, and their

*17 rue Saint Fiacre, Compiègne*

two sons, René and Marcel lived on the second floor. Mrs Clausse was a nurse at the hospital of Compiègne. She was a very kind and discreet person. Her husband worked at an auction hall. It was a big warehouse with no heat in the winter and no ventilation in summer. His work was a demanding manual job. Using a handcart, Mr Clausse collected furniture and household items from residences, loading and unloading heavy pieces all day long. He was a "down-to-earth" person always ready to help. Without knowing us, he gave my father a hand when we moved into 17 rue Saint Fiacre.

He liked talking to my father. His wife recalls that he warned my father many times about the dangers of ongoing persecution of Jews. She remembers him saying: "You and your family should go in hiding before it's too late. People are disappearing, one family at a time. You cannot trust these criminals."

While he may not have been highly educated, Mr Clausse was a very wise man who had both good common sense and vision. Even with his foresight he did not know how demented the Nazis truly were.

My father would raise his shoulders and respond, "Where can we go? The train stations and the roads are watched. Our I.D. cards show we are Jewish. Jews are not allowed to travel. I do not know how to get fake I.D. cards. Anyway, we are poor. The Germans are not interested in us. They go after the rich Jews they can steal from."

Dark clouds were accumulating.

I often played with one of the Clausses' daughters, Geneviève, in the backyard of our building. We were about the same age.

Henri and Suzanne Ribouleau were about five years older than my parents. Mr and Mrs Ribouleau always greeted us warmly whenever we met. They were kind people. They both worked as civilians for the "Aérostiers," a branch of the French Air Force that manufactured parachutes and blimps.

Their youngest son, seventeen year-old Marcel, loved my father. They got along very well. He worked for a bank. Every Sunday morning, he accompanied my Dad on his trips to the countryside where they exchanged clothes for food. Food was severely rationed. Bartering was considered "black market" and strictly forbidden by the authorities. My father and Marcel risked their freedom and perhaps their lives in order to feed the families. If caught, they could have been imprisoned, deported, even executed.

My father encouraged Marcel to eventually work for himself. Marcel dreamed of starting his own business, which he ultimately did after the war.

Marcel's brother, twenty-year-old René, worked for the French railroad company, SNCF (Société Nationale des Chemins de Fer Français.) The three families at 17 rue St Fiacre got along well. We lived in a climate of uncertainty, suspicion, and severe shortages of food and basic necessities.

Anonymous denunciations started soon after the German occupation, claiming that the people who were denounced were Communists or associated with the underground. The letters were sent to the Gestapo* headquarters. In most cases these denunciations came from people who sought revenge on their personal enemies, including neighbors, family members, coworkers, etc. The fear of being denounced lasted the duration of the war.

One Sunday in 1941 my parents had invited the Ribouleau family for dessert, probably to reinforce the bonds of neighborly friendship. They also wanted to thank them for their help in mailing packages to Uncle Charles Blum who was a prisoner of war in Germany. While all the adults were wandering around the apartment, I climbed on a chair in the kitchen and picked as many cherries as I could out of the two pies that my mother had baked for our guests! My sister Rachel has often reminded me of my being a rascal, which she found very funny. I probably was punished for this mischief.

In October 1941, I started kindergarten at the school "Saint Germain," half a mile away from home.

After the invasion of France, the first few weeks of the Occupation were oppressively calm. It felt like a blanket of fog was hovering over the town. Fear was seeping in and becoming a familiar part of life. My parents continued to work six days a week selling clothes on the open-air markets in the morning and fashioning and altering garments in the afternoon. Raw material such as fabric had also become scarce. Food and commodities of all kind were unavailable. It was difficult to get ration cards. The black-market prices kept increasing. The winters were particularly difficult. We suffered from hunger and the cold. Gasoline was no longer available. Bicycle-taxis were popular. People were resourceful.

The Germans commandeered the most beautiful properties in town. The Gestapo (SS) expelled our doctor from his home/office to install the Kommandantur headquarters for the German secret police. A large red flag with the Nazi swastika flew on top of the

---

* Gestapo: *Geheime Staatspolizei,* or secret state police of Nazi Germany and German-occupied Europe. It was administered by officers of the SS or *Schutzstaffel,* the paramilitary arm of the Nazi Party.

house. The German military police occupied former Army barracks at the Camp of Royallieu. This camp was then used to incarcerate political prisoners and resistance fighters. The first train of deportees heading for Auschwitz left Compiègne in March of 1942.

On September 27, 1940, under German orders, Jewish people were ordered to register with the Préfecture.* Along with about eight hundred other Jewish people, my parents stood in line for many hours to have their I.D. card stamped "JUIF," (Jew) and to pick up their yellow stars, a sign of infamy that would brand them and cut them off from society.

A few days later, more degrading measures were announced. Jews were now excluded from any public service functions.

On October 18, Jewish companies had to be reported to the authorities. All Jewish-owned businesses and shops were required to post a yellow sign of a required size in front of their buildings. Shortly thereafter, the companies owned by Jews were seized by the authorities and entrusted to French managers appointed by the authorities.

Throughout 1941, the following list of prohibited positions for Jewish people was published: doctors, surgeons, obstetricians, dentists, pharmacists, lawyers, notaries, and architects.

On March 25, 1941, the Pétain French government created the General Board of Jewish Inquiries. It was responsible for "Aryanisation," or ridding the French economy and culture of "non-Aryans," as well as establishing strict and restrictive anti-Jewish legislation.

In June of 1941, a new more intense and encompassing Jewish status banned Jews from holding commercial, industrial and artisan jobs, including those in the newspaper, radio, and movie industries. Offenders were to be punished with penalties, prison, deportation or death.

My father was no longer authorized to own his business. He took a job digging trenches and fixing potholes. He secretly continued to alter and make clothes at home. Miss Dervillé, a lady from Compiègne whose brother-in-law owned a men's and women's clothing store recalled the times when she would bring my father

---

* The Préfecture to this day is an administration within the Ministry of the Interior; it is in charge of the delivery of identity cards, driving licenses, passports, residency and work permits for foreigners, vehicle registration, and of the management of the police and firefighters.

clothes to be modified. My parents and Uncle Joseph shared the little work that was available.

The anti-Jewish restrictions continued:

- August 13, 1941: Jews were forbidden to hold jobs at radio stations.
- February 7, 1942: the curfew for Jews between 8 p.m. and 6 a.m. was set up.
- Jews were no longer allowed to move.
- May 29, 1942: Jews from the age of six on were required to wear a yellow star of a required size, sewn and visible at all times on the left side of their clothes.
- July 1, 1942: Jews were not allowed to use a private or public telephone.
- July 8, 1942: Jews were no longer allowed to go to a theater or any public places.
- Jews were allowed to enter stores only between 3:00 and 4:00 p.m.
- July 13, 1942: A new decree confirmed all the preceding ones and reaffirmed that Jews are excluded from all public places, including restaurants, cafés, theaters, movie theaters, public phone booths, markets, swimming pools, beaches, museums, libraries, historical monuments, race courses, etc.

Jews were now totally segregated from the non-Jewish population with no reaction from the community. How could one react? People lived in fear of the Germans and of the collaborating French administration including the police under the authority of the Vichy French government.

The French Resistance began to organize as early as November 1940. Red underground posters were seen on the walls of buildings and homes. They published pamphlets calling for resistance and fighting the "invaders." Individual initiatives were already taking place before merging ultimately into underground networks. A resident of Compiègne, Eugène Cauchois, was shot dead by the Nazis on December 4, 1941 after being accused of Underground activities and weapons possession.

Early 1941, the municipality of Compiègne, presided over by Jean Lhuillier, the mayor's third deputy, started collaborating with the Germans and the hated French government of Pétain.

Until the Germans invaded France, my parents had never felt anti-Semitism in the prior ten years. They did not actively practice religion. They did not hide their Jewish heritage, as would no one else hide their inherited religious affiliation.

My sister Rachel who was nine years old at the time never did wear the yellow star. Had she been caught, all of us would have been deported. She would walk some distance behind my parents to pretend that she was not with them. I was, fortunately, too young to wear the infamous Star of David.

Until the morning he was arrested, my father firmly believed that our family would be spared despite all the repulsive measures taken against the Jews and all the arrests. He was in denial!

How can one explain the Machiavellian process of isolating a whole segment of the population step by step so that the rest would believe that they would not be affected? Having lived ten years in France legally, my parents considered themselves French. They felt so much at home in Compiègne.

They never imagined that on July 19, 1942, the local French police would arrest them both and hand them over to the Gestapo who would send them to slavery and death.

Chapter 6

# Drancy

Drancy is a small working-class town, located in the northeastern suburbs of Paris. The Vichy government of Philippe Pétain created the Drancy internment camp in 1941, as well as many other detention centers throughout France. Drancy was under the control of the French police from 1941 to July 1943 when the Nazis took day-to-day control of all internment centers in order to feed the many extermination camps disseminated throughout Eastern Europe at an ever increasing rate. These French internment centers were effectively the "antechamber" of the death camps.

Before the war, the Drancy internment camp was intended for use as a police barracks. In 1941, it was not yet completed: many buildings were missing doors and windows, the cement floors were still under construction. The cold winter had burst many of the central heating pipes. Despite its state of disrepair, the French police authorities decided to use it as an internment camp for undesirables such as Jews, underground fighters, communists, homosexuals, hostages, and the many innocents who had been denounced or been at the wrong place during roundups. The camp was surrounded by a high wall and double row of barbed wire. The large four-story buildings formed a "U." Designed to be the home for seven hundred policemen, the facility at Drancy held up to seven thousand detainees at times.

The camp was officially opened in August 1941, shortly before the French police rounded up four thousand Jews. From that point on and throughout the war, the French police continued the roundups and the internment of "undesirables" in full cooperation with the Nazis.

The people arrested were first brought to the large courtyard of the internment center and then taken to the overcrowded dormitories. Most had to sleep on the concrete floor. Internees would stay days or weeks before being deported to death camps.

The detainees at Drancy were subjected to inhuman conditions. Food was lacking. The facilities were terribly unsanitary and overcrowded. Beds were made of rotting wooden boards with straw mattresses where two or three people slept tormented by bed bugs and lice. There were no lockers to store personal items. The toilets were in the "red castle," a brick building located in the courtyard. There were sixty toilets for up to seven thousand detainees and only twenty faucets. Privacy was nonexistent. There were some sinks in the dormitories, but water was cut off from 7 p.m. to 7 a.m. There were only two tubs in the courtyard to wash clothes. Detainees, at least those who stayed long enough, were allowed to shower once every fifteen days.

There are countless testimonies of the brutality by the French police in Drancy. Children of any age were separated upon their arrival from their parents and kept in buildings without any adult oversight or help. Many of them did not survive Drancy.

In December of 1941, forty detainees at the Drancy camp were executed in retaliation for an Underground attack on German soldiers.

In another incident, on April 6, 1944, SS Lieutenant Klaus Barbie, called "the Butcher of Lyon," led a raid on an orphanage in Izieu, a small village located at the foot of the Alps close to Lyon. He forcefully removed forty-four Jewish children and their caretakers and had them transported to Drancy. They were deported to Auschwitz. Forty-two children and five adults were gassed on arrival. The two oldest children and the superintendent of the orphanage, Miron Zlatin, were put to death by a firing squad in Tallinn, Estonia.

Food was reduced to a strict minimum: per day, two pieces of sugar, a two-pound loaf of bread for seven detainees, two cups of rutabaga soup and a scrap of meat on Sunday. There was a thriving black market inside the Drancy camp. Prices for food and necessities were exorbitant. A cup of soup cost one hundred francs; a typical average monthly salary at that time was eight hundred francs.

The French police were responsible for maintaining order among the detainees. Very few police officers displayed compassion. Many of them were involved in the black market of food and necessities. Some would steal the packages sent by families, which had been bought at great expense as food was extremely difficult to find on the outside.

The French police camp commander appointed Jewish internees to run the internal administration. The camp was divided in
sections with a detainee responsible for each stairwell. They wore
white armbands and their deputies blue armbands with a red dia-
mond. Those responsible for maintaining general order wore red
armbands. The daily schedule was made up of several roll calls,
chores, meager meals, and an hour and a half in the courtyard
where prisoners were allowed to gather. Rumors flew. The rules
were very strict. It was forbidden to wander from one staircase to
another or to visit a spouse or a friend. The main preoccupation of
the detainees—aside from constant hunger, worrying about their
families, and the horrible living conditions—was to find where
those transports were headed. That secret was well kept for the entire duration of the war. Each inmate was authorized to write and
receive two postcards a month, but most never stayed a month in
Drancy. They were also authorized to receive a parcel of food, not
to exceed five pounds, once a week, and a package of clothes twice
a month. Cigarettes, medicine, alcohol, and writing utensils were
banned. But, again, most packages never reached their intended
detainees.

New detainees came almost every day. Three times a week, on
Sundays, Tuesdays, and Thursdays, one thousand detainees plus a
back up were selected for deportation. No one knew the destination. Jews, selected by the French police, were responsible for the
selection of the deportees. It was a question of days or weeks before
their own name would be on the list.

Jews forced to select Jews!

Fewer than two thousand of the sixty-five thousand Jews deported from Drancy survived the Holocaust.

Benjamin Schatzman, a renowned author interned in Drancy,
wrote in his diary* that on July 15, 1942, there were rumors of mas-
sive arrests of Jews in Paris. Prior to this roundup, to make room
for new arrivals, up to eighty-five inmates were crammed into each
room, with four or five sleeping on the same straw-covered wooden
bed. On the morning of July 16, 1942, all internees were banned
from the courtyard. Windows and shutters were ordered closed

* Benjamin Shatzman, *Journal d'un interné: Compiègne, Drancy, Pithiviers 12
décembre 1941 – 23 septembre 1942* (Fayard, 2006)

and no one was allowed to stand by the windows. Schatzman had found a spot to watch the scene, at the risk of severe punishment. At 7:30 a.m. he saw many public Parisian city buses start arriving in the courtyard. Men and women got off the buses carrying suitcases, bundles, bags, and satchels and gathered in a hurry, not knowing where they were going. Men, women, and children were separated immediately. He wrote that the women's faces shocked him. He said they look "terrified and grief-stricken" and "their eyes wouldn't stop weeping."

On July 16 and 17, 1942, the French Police executed the orders of a German decree code-named "Vent de Printemps," "Operation Spring Breeze," and performed a mass arrest of Jews with an enthusiasm that surprised the Germans. Not one German soldier participated in this operation. Over the course of two days, 12,884 people—3,031 men, 5,802 women and 4,051 children between the ages of two and twelve—were rounded up, and herded to the "Vélodrome d'Hiver" (Vel' d'Hiv'*). All arrested, including the children, were kept there for five days without any food, medical care, water, functioning toilets, and washing facilities. After this first stop on their path toward death, they were transported to Drancy. This detention camp was even worse than the horrible conditions they had endured at the Vel' d'Hiv'. Most of the children remained in Drancy, for days and some for weeks without parents, any care and adequate food. Many babies and young children died there. Eventually the survivors were deported to Auschwitz. The ones who survived the journey were gassed and burned upon arrival. Only 811 arrested during this raid survived.

More than 6,000 Jewish children from all the regions of France were arrested and transported to their deaths between July 17 and September 30, 1942. From 1942 to 1944 more than 70,000 Jews were deported from the Drancy, Bobigny, Compiègne, Pithiviers, and Beaune-la-Rolande train stations to the Nazi extermination camps. Only 2500 survived.

It was in an atmosphere of panic and terror that our parents arrived in Drancy on July 20, 1942, according to archives at the War Veterans and War Victims Ministry.

---

* Vel' d'Hiv' is an abbreviation for "Vélodrome d'Hiver" (Winter Bicycling Indoor Stadium), where detainees were temporarily held on July 16 & 17, 1942.

My parents, Aunt Madeleine, and Uncle Joseph were arrested on the same day, July 19, 1942. Taken by complete surprise and in a terrible rush, they had to leave their three-year old son Charlot with their neighbors, the Baugis family.

My parents, uncle and aunt probably spent the night of the 19th in Compiègne at the SS headquarters before being transferred to Drancy. I can imagine their anguish upon their arrival at the Drancy internment camp, where they were separated, and upon discovering the living conditions. How long would they stay there? Will they be reunited soon with their children—my ten-year-old sister Rachel and me, only four and a half years old?

Perhaps my mother was able to stay with her sister-in-law Madeleine, and my father with his brother Joseph. All detainees arriving in Drancy were told to leave their luggage in the middle of the courtyard. They were thoroughly searched and their identity papers taken away. They did not know yet that they had ceased to be people with a name or a personality. They were handed a spoon, a fork, a metal cup, and a stale, sometimes moldy, piece of bread. In the courtyard there were mountains of baggage, piled up haphazardly. People tried to find their personal affairs as best as they could after the tiresome and degrading registration formalities were over.

About a week after our parents left our home, we received a card from Drancy dated July 27, 1942. Our mother had signed it. She had someone write it. She did not know how to write in French. It would be the only communication ever received from our parents, though it was a ray of hope that lasted until the end of the war.

In her card, my mother was asking for clothes, personal hygiene items, food and cooking utensils.

The Ribouleaus sent the package immediately with all the items requested. We learned long after the war that by the time the package reached Drancy, they had already been transported in cattle cars to Auschwitz. My mother had already been reduced to ashes, and my father had become a slave of the Reich.

My sister Rachel held onto that card dearly.

We kept on thinking that they were either still in Drancy or somewhere else in Europe, probably in Germany working in a factory. We really thought that they would be liberated after a certain time. After all, they were innocent, victims of an arbitrary arrest.

*Card from my mother written in Drancy, July 1942. It reads:*

*Madame Malmed – Drancy Camp Staircase 8, Room 10*
*Dear friends, my husband and I are in good health.*

    *Send us news of you and of our children. Now, is it possible for you to send us a small package of clothing, the following things, 1 pair of socks for my husband, black ones, 2 flannels, 2 warm night-gowns for me, 2 warm panties, 1 small saucepan, a few bars of soap, some tooth paste, 1 tooth brush, some food. You will find all of it in my cupboard. I think you will find everything. Also add for my husband yellow measuring tapes. 2 pairs of socks, the small, fancy apron – I hope that you can send this as soon as possible.*

    *I apologize and thank you in advance for this big favor – You know that you are the only ones I have. I'll pay you back one day. You can answer me with the card. Please add some hairpins and the sanitary napkin that is on the night table and for my husband, another shirt and warm underwear and tall slippers for both of us. Please tell us about our children. I kiss you as well as my little ones affectionately.*

*Card from my mother written in Drancy, July 1942. (continued)*

The night before departure, deportees were again frisked and stripped of their jewelry, money, and any other valuables. They were given a receipt in exchange for their belongings. They were told that their French money would be paid in another currency, when they arrived at their destination. They were locked up in rooms with no beds or chairs until dawn. Buckets served as toilets. During the night, singing, prayers, and sobbing could be heard in many different languages. What were my parents' thoughts that night, separated from their spouse and their children? They had no idea of where they were going. They must have feared for us, their children, not knowing whether Mr and Mrs Ribouleau would keep us or if we had already been taken away by the French police or the SS.

There were many children of all ages in Drancy, all separated from their parents. Can we imagine them, alone, lost, scared, and starving? Our parents probably wondered if we were there as well. Out of 76,000 Jews, 11,400 children, 2,000 of them less than six years old, were deported, most of them from Drancy, to extermination camps. None of them survived.

It is heart wrenching to think about the torments, the hurt, and the fear our parents must have felt. They must have been shocked and outraged by the hate and brutality they were experiencing at the hands of the French authorities.

They were deported from Drancy to Auschwitz on July 29, 1942. At dawn, public buses picked them up and drove them to the Bobigny or Bourget train stations. Probably, like their unfortunate companions, my parents held onto a glimmer of hope that they would one day soon return home and see us once again reunited, at least until the cattle car doors slammed shut. They were in Convoy № 12.

That train transported two hundred and seventy men and seven hundred thirty women.

There were rumors of ghettos and forced labor work camps. In the absence of any other information, the deportees talked about a mysterious place they called "Pitchipoi,"* an imagined place where they would be reunited with their family after leaving Drancy. Very few, if any, thought they were being transported to their death.

The real "Pitchipoi," turned out to be a place where they would meet death upon arrival or worse, they would become slaves. The survivors of that initial selection would suffer and eventually die from starvation, exhaustion, torture, and sickness or from the bullet of an SS guard looking for fun. Or it might be from the gas chamber and the cremation oven to keep the daily deaths quotas and make room for the people arriving the next day in cattle cars from all over Europe.

July 1942 was a very hot summer month. A hundred or more deportees were piled into each train car with practically no air, no food, only one bucket of water, and one bucket for hygiene, which was inaccessible to most. There was no room to sit. Lying down would be death as one would quickly be trampled. These infernal journeys lasted for at least three days, sometimes five.

Could my mother have survived such conditions? Was she smothered or trampled to death? Was she alone? Was she with my father? Was she with my Aunt Madeleine? How did they fare? My father was strong. He was courageous. How can one survive three plus days of standing up, bodies against bodies with no water, no food, no possibility to defecate or to urinate in 90°F-plus heat. Did thirst, hunger and despair drive deportees to madness?

Two to three hundred people out of one thousand deportees died during each transport and many went insane.

On convoy № 12, two hundred sixty nine men who arrived at Auschwitz were tattooed "54153" to "54422." My father was number "54315." My mother, if she had actually survived the three or four-day infernal journey, was not given a number according to the re-

---

* "Pitchipoi" is the imaginary place where Jews in the Drancy internment camp believed they would be deported to. For some, Pitchipoi was the nonsense name of a Polish ghetto; for some, the word was like an eternal curse; for others, Pitchipoi was a place of compulsory forced labor. It was Nazi policy to keep Jewish prisoners in a state of ignorance about their final destination, so Pitchipoi was invented to fill the vacuum.

cords, which implied she was gassed and burned upon arrival. In this convoy all the men entered the slave camp. Two hundred sixteen women were immediately gassed and burned, probably alive.

After standing in the cattle car, for days, among dead people, I can imagine the terror of the deportees when the SS unlocked the doors of the cattle cars at their arrival in Auschwitz or at any other death camp. They were brutally pulled out, hit with truncheons and rifle butts, and screamed at with insults while the dogs barked savagely and bit them.

On arrival at the extermination camps, the adults and teenagers who passed the selections were enslaved to work twelve-hour shifts, living on less than three hundred calories per day. Most died from starvation, exhaustion, or sickness weeks or months after arrival. Very few survived a year or two.

Soon after, they disappeared into another world—as if no man or woman called Srul and Chana Malmed had ever lived, loved, laughed, cried, sung, and hoped. Whisked away from the land of the living, they no longer had the right to exist. They became numbers, anonymous slaves of the Reich where the SS had the power to let them live or to murder and torture them with impunity.

Altogether, between the first transport of August 1941 and the last on July 31, 1944, 64,759 Jews were deported from Drancy in 64 train transports. Approximately 61,000 of them were sent to Auschwitz-Birkenau. 3,753 were sent to the Sobibor extermination camp. Less than 2,000 deported from the Drancy camp survived the Holocaust.

Chapter 7

# Henri and Suzanne Ribouleau

My sister and I sprang into the lives of Henri and Suzanne Ribouleau on July 19, 1942.

When Henri and Suzanne Ribouleau were still alive, I did not ask the questions that might stir painful memories and be upsetting to them and to myself. We practically never brought up the past out of modesty, fear of unleashing emotions. We were afraid to wake up ghosts.

As it is with all people we love dearly, I wanted them to be immortal. I knew they would be gone one day and I dreaded that day. Fortunately, they lived a relatively long life. Papa Henri died at the age of eighty-four and Maman Suzanne at ninety-eight.

I was sixty years old when I finally felt that I could control my emotions and was able to speak about the war times. It was almost too late. Papa Henri was no longer with us. Maman Suzanne was in an advanced stage of Alzheimer's disease. Unfortunately, the disease had erased most of the detailed answers that interested me about my parents, Papa Henri, and Maman Suzanne's younger years.

Some information, I do recall. Papa Henri was born to a poor family in 1901 in Bracieux near Blois. When he was twelve years old, he began working as a rope maker. Ropes were commonly used for any work that required lifting and pulling, such as harnesses for horses. Horses were the major means of transportation and farm work. Papa Henri's skills in rope making got him a civilian position with an Air Force division called Aérostation where airships and parachutes were manufactured.

Maman Suzanne was slightly younger than Papa Henri. Her maiden name was Mouton. She was born in 1905 also into a poor family. As a child, she walked to and from school every day seven miles each way, summers and winters. Due to the dire financial sit-

*Maman and Papa Henri Ribouleau, 1972*

uation of her family, Maman Suzanne had to quit school at the age
of ten. She went to live with a wealthy family as a servant without
pay, for room and board only. She was there for a number of years.
She learned to sew and became a gifted seamstress. Her adult I.D.
card showed her profession as "shoemaker technician." It is possible
that at one time she was employed in a shoe factory.

Papa Henri and Maman Suzanne were married in 1922. Both were employed at the Aérostiers in the town of Saint-Cyr-l'Ecole on the outskirts of Paris. They remained there until the French Air Force transferred them to another manufacturing facility in Compiègne, about forty miles north of Paris, in the 1930s. They rented the second-floor apartment at 17 rue Saint Fiacre.

When my sister and I moved in with them in 1942, I remember admiring their elegant dining room. My parents could not afford dining room furniture. I was fascinated by the dark, almost black, wooden buffet with many intricate carved turrets. It looked like a medieval castle. I spent many hours playing at the bottom of this "fortress."

On July 19, 1942, after our parents had left with the gendarmes, with my sister Rachel holding my hand tight, we descended the stairs from the third to the second floor where the Ribouleau family lived. As she was leaving, my mother had handed me a jar of butter, a rare commodity in those days of severe shortages. As we entered the apartment, I handed the jar to Madame Ribouleau. She thanked me and, affectionately, held me tight against her. I was sobbing, unable to stop. Rachel remained silent. We were all in a state of shock. *What had just happened on this sunny Sunday morning?* We remained in the kitchen a long time, distraught and unable to decide what to do next. *How could I understand? Why were my parents taken away? When will they be back?*

"They will be back. It is a mistake," Henri Ribouleau repeated several times.

"This war is bringing so much misery! Why would anyone arrest such good people, honest, hard working, good parents with two wonderful children? What have they done?" asked Mrs Ribouleau.

Rachel courageously held back her tears. I continued to sob and called out for my parents. I hardly knew these neighbors. Were we going to stay with them? Mrs Ribouleau sat down and tried to reassure us by gently speaking to us. She had a regional accent we were not familiar with. Mr and Mrs Ribouleau and their two sons, twenty-two year old René and twenty-year old Marcel were very kind to us. Everything was quiet except for my whimpering. We were all overwhelmed by the events and by grief. The day went by without any news of our parents. We stayed pinned to our chairs not knowing what to do. Thoughts were racing in our heads. When we heard footsteps in the street, we hurried to the window full of hope.

When evening came, we had to get organized, at least for one night we thought. There wasn't enough room for the six of us in the second floor apartment. It was decided that René and Marcel would go and sleep in our parents' apartment. They did not know that they would sleep there every single night, for almost the next three years.

René and Marcel's first night in our parents' apartment was July 19, 1942. All believed that this situation would last only a few days.

"The Malmeds will be back any day," Mr Ribouleau kept saying.

In the meantime, my small bed was set up in Mr and Mrs Ribouleau's bedroom, while Rachel moved into the bedroom René and Marcel had vacated.

In July, Rachel was on school holidays. Mr and Mrs Ribouleau arranged their schedule so that we wouldn't be alone during the day. We became part of the family. René and Marcel treated us like their brother and sister, even though we monopolized some of their parents' affection. We moved in their room; we shared the small space they lived in and deprived them of some of the food that they needed badly at their age. We certainly disrupted their existence and they accepted us like we had been there all the time.

The Ribouleau family earned a very modest income, barely sufficient to feed and take care of six people. Because of their sudden and unexpected arrest, our parents did not leave any money in the apartment. As a result of the few words my father had mumbled when they were arrested, it was suspected that they had kept hidden some money in the garage, in case. It was never found. So sure that my parents would come back, the Ribouleaus continued to pay my parents' apartment rent for close to three years.

Despite the Ribouleau's affection, my sister and I remained worried. We were too traumatized by the brutal separation from our parents to bond immediately with these kind and reassuring strangers. I was no longer the spoiled child, the little prince of the Malmeds, but a timid and silent little boy of almost five years old, who woke up screaming every morning at 5:00 a.m. It took weeks before I started to speak again.

My sister and I behaved like zombies. Apprehension and fear were with us all the time. Our cozy nest had been destroyed. We tried, not very successfully, to hide our pain and avoid burdening this caring family. We were worried that they would not keep us or even separate us. What would happen to us? We had nowhere to go and no one to go to. We realized how much of a burden we were. And we were Jewish. Although I didn't understand the meaning of this word, I knew that it was full of threats. The Ribouleaus were taking considerable risks by keeping us. Besides the Clausses, a very discreet family, who lived on the ground floor of our building, some neighbors began to express their concern. They would tell the Ribouleaus:

"Aren't you afraid to hide these Jewish children? You risk being arrested, deported or shot."

Others would add:

"When the war is over, they'll go back to their parents. You will never hear from them again. You will be lucky if they even thank you."

Our presence bothered these neighbors. They were afraid for their own security. They would have liked for us to move away from their street.

The Ribouleaus kept replying.

"We promised their parents that we would look after them. We will keep our promise."

They kept their promise.

It was strictly forbidden to give shelter, help, or hide Jewish people of any age. The penalty was imprisonment, probably torture, and deportation, or being shot in the nearby forest. The fear of being denounced weighed heavily on all of us and all who knew about us.

It took me some time to start feeling comfortable with the Ribouleaus. Several months after we moved in, one evening after dinner I spontaneously climbed onto Mr Ribouleau's knees and called him "Papa." It was a very emotional moment for all around the table I was told. From then on, I began to call these two wonderful people "Papa" and "Maman." I was still thinking about my parents, and I still do to this day. Rachel called them "Uncle Henri" and "Aunt Suzanne." Although she was only ten years old, she cared for me affectionately like a mother does.

Maman Suzanne was happy to have a girl in the family. She made clothes for Rachel and taught her how to sew, knit, cook, and clean. When Rachel didn't behave and deserved a punishment, she was given handkerchiefs to hem. She always completed her tasks. As for me, I played with the wooden logs piled in a basket close to the stove.

Gradually, we fell into routines and behaved like we had always lived there. We became part of the Ribouleau family at large. All the uncles, aunts, nieces, and friends of the family we lived with considered us like their nephew and niece and cousins.

In the morning, I liked watching Marcel as he carefully combed his hair before going to work. He had an unusual routine. He used salad oil to sculpt and make his jet-black wavy hair shine!

Since we were in hiding, my sister and I did not have any ration cards. Ration cards were the only way to get any food from the grocery stores. The six of us had to subsist on four cards, which would have meant near starvation without our gardens. Several times a week Papa Henri would get up early to stand in line at 4:00 a.m. at the butcher or the fish store. When he returned empty-handed, our plates were filled with food we didn't like, like spinach from the garden. Despite the severe food restrictions worsening as the war went on, Papa Henri and Maman Suzanne made sure that we always had something to eat. The four of them had to deprive themselves of food for us, the two children who were not even related and practically strangers.

Papa Henri and Maman Suzanne had promised our parents to take care of us. The dangers and the starvation diets made it difficult to survive. And yet ...

Would they keep their promise?

Chapter 8

# Our Schools

I started nursery school in autumn of 1942. I was five years old. From the time our parents were taken away to the time we started school, Rachel and I were never alone. Maman Suzanne stayed home with us. All this time, I was not allowed to go and play outdoors. I played quietly in the kitchen with wood logs, crayons, and old newspapers while Maman Suzanne sewed, washed, ironed, cleaned the two apartments, and prepared the meals with whatever she had available.

I have no memory of my first day at school. I suppose that Maman Suzanne took me to the "Saint-Germain" kindergarten. There were three schools next to each other: the kindergarten, the girls' school, and a separate boys' school. Starting the second day, Rachel accompanied me in the morning and brought me back home in the afternoon. She was always watching over me with concern and love. Neither one of us wore the yellow star. Rachel was violating the law, as people older than nine had to wear the Star of David.

In school, most kids wore a grey smock. We blended in. Every morning there was a roll call in the classroom. When the teacher called "Malmed," I felt anxiety and fear that someone would comment and say the word Jew.

When Papa Henri was not working at his day job, he was either collecting wood in the forest for the kitchen stove or working the three small gardens, weather permitting, or going to the fields to cut some grass for the few rabbits, chicken and ducks or going to the farms around us to try to buy a few eggs, poultry, and anything that was eatable. He was constantly worried about not being able to feed his enlarged family. One of his many tasks was replacing the worn out soles of our shoes. He used pieces of old bike tires, which he glued or nailed down to the soles of the shoes.

For the longest time, I was a shy and nearly mute child who lived in constant fear of being separated from this caring family.

The slightest noise made me jump. A change in the tone of voices scared me. I was so afraid that the gendarmes would come back to get us. Until the end of the war, I continued to be afraid, even terrorized and overwhelmed with fear whenever I saw a policeman.

All people of Jewish faith including children had been registered with the Prefecture at the beginning of the Occupation. Knowing that, it must have weighed heavily on Papa and Maman Ribouleau' shoulders.

But the promise they had made to our parents to protect us was sacred for them.

No matter what, Papa Henri and Maman Suzanne would keep their word.

The days were monotonous and filled with the fear, bursts of hope and moments of sadness. My love for the ones I now called Papa and Maman was growing. We kept hoping and waiting for another card or letter from our parents.

Papa Henri and Maman Suzanne did not dare contact the authorities to find out the status of our parents for fear of attracting attention. *Where could they be?*

Several times a week, a long line of prisoners looking miserable, frail and dirty, carrying a suitcase or a bundle marched on the main street going to or from the Compiègne train station two miles away. The Royallieu Internment Camp was located less than half a mile from where we lived. We could not help, but hoped to see our parents among these poor people.

They were alive—we didn't even think of any other possibilities—and they would come back soon.

To go to school, we had no choice but to walk on the "rue de Paris," the main street that connected the center of the town with the Royallieu internment camp, and always busy with German soldiers on foot, motorcycles, cars, or trucks. I walked close to the houses or the fences. I was trying to meld with them hoping to become invisible. This twice-a-day walk was a real ordeal. When a truck, a car, or a motorcycle slowed down near us, I was sure that we were going to be arrested. Paralyzed with fright, I clung to my sister's hand as she made sure we continued to walk. And I did so mechanically, one foot in front of the other, until I reached my refuges, the school or our home.

Even at home or in school, I never felt safe. Our attendance at school was frequently interrupted when we heard any suspicious rumors of a roundup. Papa and Maman Ribouleau would keep us at home hidden in the basement.

At one time, I did not go to school due to a potential roundup and missed an important test. When I came back a day or two later, the teacher had failed me. I explained why I was not in class the day of the test and asked him if I could take it. He refused angrily.

*But ... why, sir? I asked. I can take the test right now if you let me. I have studied for it and I am confident I can pass.*

"No, you were absent. You failed. Sit down," he said, irritated.

I was eight or nine years old. I didn't insist. However, to this day, I remember the despair and the extreme sense of injustice that I wished I could have expressed, but I didn't want to draw attention to myself. I had the feeling, rightly or wrongly, that some of the teachers were uncomfortable with me in their classroom. They all knew I was Jewish, and I feared that one of them would report me. I needed their encouragement so badly. I needed some sign of understanding. They never did give me any. My presence in their classroom endangered their own safety.

The boys' school was around the corner from the girls' school and the kindergarten, on "Boulevard Gambetta," a street lined with old chestnut trees. Every autumn, the boys had chestnut fights. In winter, there was always snow. The homeowners cleared a path on the sidewalk in front of their house. We had wonderful times sliding on the ice that collected in the gutters. I can still hear the children's happy cries during the recesses. We played tag chasing each other around all over the playground. One other favorite game was called "motorcycle." It required two people. The one in the back, the driver, held his partner in front called the engine. Both would run as fast as possible chasing other teams. We also played with red clay marbles. On the other side of the wall separating the boys and girls courtyards, the girls played hopscotch and jump rope. We would return to the classroom, red-faced and out of breath.

During the recesses, the war seemed far away. Interestingly, no one talked about the war. It was considered taboo. I guess our teachers did not want to add more fear to our daily life, which was already heavily burdened by the daily miseries at home.

A few days a week, the Red Cross distributed a glass of milk and a cookie mid-afternoon.

Among kids, we had arguments about Santa Claus. I naively believed in Santa, even though he hardly brought me anything! Some even said he didn't exist. I was convinced they were lying and it made me angry.

All the schools were under the jurisdiction of the Vichy French Government* of Pétain. A large portrait of General Philippe Pétain, Chief of State, hung on the wall at the back of the classroom. Once a day, we had to sing "Maréchal nous voilà," "Marshal here we are" and other supposedly patriotic songs that did not make sense to any of us. I sang along with the other children.

The father of one of my classmates was a small business owner. He emptied cesspools and septic tanks. He was a brave and courageous man. He often helped internees at the Royallieu camp where he had to go on a regular basis. He smuggled messages at great risk, back and forth. If caught, he would have been deported or shot. Children in school made fun of his son because of his father's line of work. He didn't know how to answer them back or where to hide. He walked, his shoulders hunched, overwhelmed by the children's mockery. Luckily I do not recall any one making fun of my situation. I felt a strong bond with this friend.

Rachel also had some good friends. Marie Lesueur, very calm and shy, was her confidante. There was Ginette Coppée, who lived across the street. We often walked to school together. Ginette was an only child with very strict parents. There was also Micheline Vallée. She lived on our street. Her father repaired radios for a living. Rachel spent many hours at Micheline's home. With her friends, Rachel was able to forget the hardship of the war and be an almost normal kid.

My sister's best friend Marie lived on one of the four streets that bordered the camp.

Rachel was a pretty girl who always smiled despite the constant fear. She was having a hard time getting used to living with strangers in a new environment and learning new habits. Maman Suzanne asked her to help with the household chores, like washing the dishes, the cleaning of the apartments, the sewing. She

---

* Following the military defeat of France and the vote by the National Assembly on July 10, 1940, Marshal Philippe Pétain was given extraordinary powers. He then established the Vichy government that administered both the German-occupied northern zone and the unoccupied southern zone of France until August 1944.

had not done any of this with our parents. Rachel was very obedient and willing to help, but occasionally she rebelled. There were a few conflicts between her and Maman Suzanne. Rachel had been getting a weekly magazine "Lisette" and she wanted a second one named "Fillettes." She had been used to our parents never saying no to things she asked for, I suppose. She was angry when Maman Suzanne said no, probably due to a tight budget. Rachel remembers, with regret saying to Maman Suzanne, "You do not want to buy me this magazine because I am not your daughter!"

Rachel and I never talked together about our parents, but they were always on our minds and in our hearts. It was an emotional subject. We had put them in a cocoon that we did not want to disturb. Asking questions would have been too painful and too emotional. If I tried, I could not have completed the sentence without breaking down.

I was studious and I did not speak much. My sister was always lively and talkative. In class photos, she always smiled. Rachel's smile might have been slightly exaggerated to look happy, be like everyone else and again not attract attention. She told her classmates that our parents were traveling and that the Ribouleaus were our Uncle and Aunt. I am not sure if all believed that tale. I never talked about my parents and no one ever asked me questions.

In the evening, we would do our homework on the kitchen table. Papa Henri helped us as best as he could. Neither Maman Suzanne nor he had a school diploma. Marcel and René had earned the "Certificat d'Etudes" which was the diploma obtained at the age of fourteen. When Rachel finished her homework, she would read her magazine or do some sewing. For at least a year, despite all the affection of my new family, I would cry myself to sleep.

Due to the lack of soap and cleaning material, lice and other diseases proliferated throughout the country for the duration of the war. Red Cross representatives came to our school once a month and inspected each one of us. When lice were found, the child's hair was shaved immediately. Maman Suzanne inspected us regularly as well, usually a day or two before the Red Cross inspection. When she saw lice, she carefully removed the eggs and the larvae.

One day after one of the official inspection, I came home from school with my "beret" pulled all the way down to my ears. No hair was showing. As soon as Rachel saw me, she began to scream.

"They shaved Leon's hair!"

She hastily removed my "beret" and, relieved, burst out laughing when she realized that I still had my dark curls! She had fallen for my prank.

In 1944, the "St. Germain" school, along with other schools in town, were requisitioned by German troops and converted into military hospitals. Our classes were transferred to empty apartments close by. With coal and wood scarce, the classrooms were rarely heated. Winters were cold. We had to keep our coats and gloves on.

When children misbehaved in class or didn't complete their homework, some teachers would send them in the hallway wearing a paper hat that was called "bonnet d'âne," "donkey's hat." They had to stand there with the hat on their heads next to the classroom door until the class was over. All children passing by would make fun of them.

I was lucky to escape that humiliation.

When would we have a normal life again?

# Chapter 9

# Our Daily Life

Maman Suzanne spent a good part of her Saturdays, doing the laundry for six people. A staircase led down to the laundry room next to the cellars. The room was lit by natural light coming from two small windows near the ceiling and at ground level in the courtyard. A sink was attached to a wall. A gas stove rested on the bare ground. A medium size round tub sat on top. Another large round tub used for the washing and the rinsing sat on a wooden tripod. Moving the boiling water from the stove to the washing tub was dangerous and backbreaking. Along with the clothes, there were the heavy bed sheets to scrub, rinse, wring the water out, and then hang them on an outdoor wire in the garden. Saturdays were exhausting. I am sure that Maman Suzanne must have thought about the extra work Rachel and I gave her.

The soap used for everything in the household was called Savon de Marseille. Even this poor-quality soap was rationed. The bar of soap was a mixture of fatty acids and sawdust.

Rachel and I did our best to help her with the Saturday chores. We did wring the clothes and sheets and helped her hang the wash on the clotheslines.

The laundry room was not heated. The only heat came from the stove while the water for the wash was being heated, but it was quickly dispersed in this drafty basement. Maman Suzanne would struggle with numb and sore fingers.

After Rachel and I started school, Maman Suzanne went back to work for the French Air Force, now under German command, sewing parachutes. In addition to long working days, she had to prepare the meals, iron the clothes, make the beds, and clean two apartments. We all helped. Maman Suzanne never complained of the extra work Rachel and I imposed on her. We all came home for lunch. Despite all this work, she still found time, I don't know how, to sew and knit.

Since it was impossible to find knitting material, Maman Suzanne unraveled old sweaters. During the unraveling process, I helped by rolling up the wool into a ball, a job I took seriously. The wool was then wrapped around my two extended arms at shoulder-width distance. Then it was washed. Once dried, we would roll it into six-inch-diameter balls to uncurl it. And out of these old sweaters she knitted sweaters and scarves, which were like new to us. Maman Suzanne also made clothes out of second-hand blankets that Papa Henri would buy on the black market. Those blankets were military khaki. After they were dyed, she fashioned them into coats, jackets, overcoats, and skirts. Her sewing machine proved invaluable during those times of hardship.

Once a year, all mattresses were refurbished. A lady we called "matelassière," a mattress maker, would bring some complex apparatus into the courtyard. This equipment was very intriguing. It looked very much like some torture rack. Each mattress was disassembled. I was fascinated by the amount of sheep-wool that came out. All mattress material was washed and dried. Using the "torture rack," the mattress maker carded the wool to bring it back to its original suppleness. I watched this unusual process from a safe distance. The mattresses were, by the end of the day, reassembled and sewn back together. They looked like new.

Family life was well organized. Each one of us had his/her chores: peeling vegetables, sweeping, waxing the bedroom and dining room wood floors, cleaning, lighting the fire, bringing up the wood or potatoes from the cellar. Rachel and I instinctively felt guilty about the extra burden we brought to the household. Our safety depended on all of them.

I was responsible for getting the groceries. Every late afternoon, I went to the grocery store with a list. It was half a block away from our home. There was always a long line of people extending to the sidewalk. The wait could be as much as one hour. I often came home with half or less of what Maman had asked, either because I did not have enough ration stamps or the products were not available.

We bought bread daily. I walked to the bakery, about a mile

from our home. Mr Hubac, the baker, a kind person, had emigrated to France from Spain. He always handed me an extra piece of bread that I ate on the way home. "Here, my boy," he would say, winking and smiling at me. "Thank you, sir," I'd answer.

The bread tasted delicious to me though the adults complained about it.

I was hungry and in addition, I did not know the difference between good and not-so-good bread, since I was too young to remember the pre-war bread. To replace the flour, only available in limited quantities, bran and sawdust were used. The same bran was fed to pigs and was also used to manufacture soap.

I would hold the loaf of bread very carefully against my chest as I left the bakery. Mr Hubac looked at me with compassion knowing my situation. *Somehow, I felt embarrassed. Why? To this day, it is difficult to explain. I guess I did not want to be different and feel the pity.*

It was also customary to get the meat daily, since there was no refrigeration at home. Mr Legrand, the butcher, lived at the corner of our street and the rue de Paris. He had two boys Maurice, the eldest, and Jacques. Papa Henri several times a week stood in line at the fish market for two to three hours before it opened. He would get up around three or four in the morning trying to make as little noise as possible. Most of the time he came home empty-handed. One time he came home very proudly with a piece of fish wrapped in newspapers.

"Look, everyone!" he said loudly, emphasizing his pleasure with a hand gesture.

He set his package on the table and removed the paper. We all huddled around, excited. I stood on tiptoes to be able to see. A strong odor of ammonia stung our nostrils.

"This fish has a bad smell, it smells like urine" said Maman Suzanne, her fists on her hips.

"Ugh! It must be spoiled! It certainly wasn't caught yesterday," she added.

"Really, you think so?" Papa Henri wondered, frowning as he looked at his prize with disappointment.

"I think that's normal; all salt water fish have this odor," he added.

Neither Rachel nor I said a word. We were all so hungry. Maman Suzanne took the smelly fish, rinsed it a long time, put it in a large saucepan full of hot water and cooked it with available seasoning.

That day, we were treated to what we thought was a delicious meal, our bellies were full, and no one got sick.

To be able to feed the family, Papa Henri cultivated three vegetable gardens. One behind our apartment building; another one about two miles away, close to the river "Oise" and one at "Maison Blanche" (White House) on the rue de Paris, across from the Internment camp. In the spring and summer we grew all kinds of vegetables such as potatoes, tomatoes, carrots, radishes, lettuce, and rutabagas. Being able to keep some of the harvest throughout the long winter without refrigeration was a challenge. Potatoes were kept in the darkest corner of the cellar so they wouldn't sprout too fast.

Due to the lack of insecticides and any other means of fighting infestation, our crops faced a danger, beetles. This pest attacked and devastated potato plants. They multiplied very quickly. The only way to keep these pests under control was to handpick them from the leaves of the potato plants one by one twice a day. This was not the most enjoyable activity!

After school and on weekends, I accompanied Papa Henri to our different gardens. To go to the garden called "La Maison Blanche" we had to walk by the Internment Camp. We walked on the opposite side of the street. Civilians were not allowed to walk on the sidewalk bordering the camp. The Internment camp was surrounded with high walls made out of thick wood boards, topped with barbed wire. There were many guard towers all around the camp. German soldiers armed with machine guns, a frightening sight, guarded the sidewalk on the camp side. The whole area was referred to as "La Maison blanche" due to the one home, painted white, in the middle of the gardens.

I held onto Papa Henri's hand so tightly that it probably was hurting.

He always whispered softly "Don't be afraid, Leon. I'm here. You're safe."

After going through this first obstacle, another one was awaiting me. To access our garden, we had to pass by the Maison Blanche where a flock of geese was roaming freely. As soon as they saw us, they came running toward me, flapping their wings furiously and trying to nip at my bare calves. I was convinced that the Germans had trained them to be nasty. I couldn't run fast enough to keep them away from me; my heart was pounding hard. Out of the three gardens, this was the one I really did not want to go to.

At one of the corners of our street "Saint Fiacre and Saint Germain," two hundred yards from our home, was a farm that belonged to a Dutchman. Each evening around six o'clock Rachel and I would walk there to buy fresh milk. My sister usually held the aluminum milk can. She sometimes let me carry it, and I felt she was doing me a big favor by trusting me with it. We walked along the wall of the farm covered with moss and spider webs. For fun, we dragged our feet on the bare ground. The entrance to the farm was around the corner at "rue Saint Germain."

We would enter the farm through a high arched porch. Its doors were always open. We then had to cross a large, often muddy courtyard cluttered with farming equipment. Two huge black German shepherds roamed the courtyard. They barked ferociously as we passed, showing their teeth, looking like they were ready to attack us. Almost every evening, as we entered the courtyard, we saw one or two German army motorcycles with a sidecar parked near the front door of the main house.

"Look," I would whisper in my sister's ear while pointing a trembling finger toward the motorbikes. "They're here."

"Be quiet and don't point," Rachel would order me.

We could not turn around. Our family needed the milk. I held on tight to my sister's hand as we came closer to the entry door, with my head down and my heart pounding. The door opened into a large room with a long table on the right and another small table on the left with several tall milk cans. The farmer and several German soldiers would be sitting around the table on the right with glasses and wine bottles in front of them laughing and speaking German. They all had rosy cheeks and seemed kind of drunk. As we entered they looked at us. We quickly went to the left where the farmer's spouse was standing without a smile ever behind the table ready to fill our milk cans.

Rachel and I were terrified that the farmer in his half drunken state would tell his German soldier friends that we were Jewish. He was a tall man with a long, red face. Whenever I saw him standing I noticed that he always wore high rubber boots that would go up to his knees. His wife, always dressed in a black smock, looked unhappy. She stood in the same spot every day. She kept on looking at her husband getting drunk with the hated soldiers. She filled our one-quart milk can, without ever smiling or saying a word. We paid quickly. We were in a hurry to leave. But we didn't dare run, making sure we didn't attract attention. Rachel and I passed by the dogs again as fast as we could. At any moment we expected the soldiers to order us to stop and to arrest us. We regained our composure only after turning the corner of "rue Saint Germain" and "rue Saint Fiacre." We had to go through that ordeal almost daily.

On the side of our building Papa Henri kept a large pile of wood. It was about forty feet long by six feet high. He brought the wood back from the forest two to three miles away using a large two-wheeled handcart equipped with a home-made harness that was attached to the cart and strapped around his chest. René and Marcel often helped him. I went along on these foraging expeditions and trotted by the cart.

The kitchen wood stove was lit every morning. It was used to cook and to heat the kitchen where all of us lived when we were not sleeping. A second stove in the dining room was lit only during the winter on Sundays and holidays. Most of the time, the doors leading to the hallway remained closed.

The bedrooms were very cold in winter. An hour before we went to bed, bricks were heated in the kitchen oven. Rubber bladders were filled with hot water. The hot bricks wrapped in a towel and the warm bladders were slid between the humid and ice-cold bed sheets.

At the end of the garden, there was a small chicken coop where we raised three to four hens, a couple of ducks, and five to six rabbits. The hens were kept alive for as long as they laid eggs. Eventually they ended up in a pot. To feed the rabbits we had to collect dandelions and grass on the roadsides and in the fields. Every now and then Papa Henri would kill one of our rabbits for a Sunday or a holiday meal. What a feast! The aroma spread throughout the whole building. Undoubtedly the smell stirred up the neighbors' envy. Such an event was exceptional!

As I write these lines I close my eyes and I can still remember the wonderful smell of the rabbit simmering in the cast-iron pot on the stove. I have at times ordered rabbit in a restaurant when available on the menu with the expectation that I would taste Maman Suzanne's cooking again. I have always been disappointed. I have never found that very special flavor I remember so well.

In those days nothing was thrown away. Rabbit skins would be sold to "Père Lapinpeaux (Father Rabbit skin)." Once or twice a month, this old man with abundant white hair and a long moustache came to our street sitting on the bench of his one-horse-drawn carriage. He chanted as he slowly moved:

"Skins ... rabbit skins! Skins ... rabbit skins!"

All the children, whose family had been lucky to eat a rabbit, would run to his cart, holding up their dried rabbit skins. He gave them a coin in exchange for the skins.

"Thank you, sir!" we would scream, proud of the change we were careful not to lose.

For a special holiday it was decided that a duck would be killed. A two-foot high tree trunk used for that purpose stood permanently in the courtyard. Papa Henri brought the duck from the chicken coop and placed it on the trunk while holding its head with one hand and an axe in the other. Our neighbor, Marcel Clausse, was helping out by holding firmly the duck's legs. I carefully stood a few yards away, my back against the wall of our building as I watched with some apprehension the duck's execution. Papa swung the axe and decapitated the duck with a fast and steady motion. Both men let go of the unfortunate headless victim. To our amazement and dismay, the headless duck flew away toward the back of the garden.

"The duck! The duck is escaping!" everyone screamed.

We all ran and followed the duck flying about twenty feet above us. It flew over the wall of the garden and disappeared into the large field.

"Where is it? Damn it!" Papa Henri was screaming.

The decapitated bird was never found! We ate vegetables that day. The story went down in the memory book of the Ribouleau and Malmed families.

Once or twice a week we would go fishing in two small lakes known as "Etangs de Saint-Pierre," about ten miles away from home in the middle of the forest, or on the banks of the Oise River. Most of the time we would catch enough fish for dinner and sometimes on lucky days, for another day or two. Our fishing ended when German soldiers had different ideas of fishing. They began using hand grenades, rapidly depleting the fish population and depriving us of an important food supply and precious moments of peace and relaxation so sorely needed.

Papa Henri knew the forest well. On weekends in the fall we would go and look for mushrooms, which made for delicious omelets.

After a rainy night, we would go early in the morning to look for snails which were abundant in some areas that were kept secret and known only by a few.

All of this was necessary to keep food on the table.

The days, weeks, months, and years went by while we waited for the Liberation of France and the return of our parents.

Maman Suzanne and Papa Henri were constantly worried about issues like food for the next meal, heating, clothes, and most critical, the constant fear of denunciation.

The Germans had confiscated all motorized vehicles after the occupation. Maman Suzanne and Papa Henri did not own a car before the war. They used their bikes to go to work. Bikes were a luxury.

Among numerous restrictions, our life was also ruled by the curfew from 8:00 p.m. to 7:00 a.m.

The only outside news we received was from the radio. Though it was strictly forbidden to tune to Radio London, every evening at 7:00 p.m., adults listened with their ears close to the radio. Almost nightly, General de Gaulle spoke. His address always started with: "Français, Françaises" (Frenchmen, French women). He was the voice of hope. Radio London broadcast many messages in Morse code or plain encoded messages addressed to the Resistance fighters. It also broadcasted messages to boost the morale of the population. A few days after the Allied Forces landed in Italy and then in Normandy, we started to record on a map their position with tacks of different colors to mark their advances. This daily activity was very important to our psyche. It was also a great conversation and speculation piece among adults. When we started to see the Allied Forces making substantial gains, we knew that the Germans would be defeated. But how long would it take?

Soon, our parents would come home. That was our dearest hope and thought as we fell asleep.

When? Would I remember them?

Chapter 10

# Rare Peaceful Moments

In 1944, life was becoming extremely tense and difficult, living in constant fear of being denounced. Not knowing where our parents were was difficult to bear. However, between the roundups that we managed to avoid and the terrifying rumors, I was able to have fun with my friends in our street. I was a normal little kid who enjoyed playing with marbles, running behind my hoop, or trying to fly a kite. I made my own toys. An old bike rim became a hoop. I built kites with sticks made of hazel tree branches and used wrapping paper or old newspapers. I built and destroyed many kites on their maiden flights. I would fly them between our building and the neighbors' house where a draft would help them take off until they reached a certain height and would end up crashing against a wall. I would either repair them or, more often, build a new one hoping that the improvements would help it clear the roof of our building.

We had hoop races. Occasionally, we lost control of our hoops, and they would land in the middle of the girls' games. They would scream at us for interrupting their hopscotch games or rope jumping. They loved to make fun of us boys when they saw us red-faced and sweaty with our bicycle rims or our broken kites. Sometimes, a German truck or motorcycle would turn on our street and interrupt our joyful plays. The ten or twenty children at play would fly away like a flock of sparrows and disappear into secret hideouts.

For Christmas or Easter, Papa and Maman Ribouleau would often invite Mr and Mrs Renouard, their favorite friends. They had met when Papa and Maman Ribouleau lived and worked near Paris, and they remained friends for life. The Renouards lived in Viroflay, a small town in the suburbs of Paris. They came to Compiègne by train. We admired their "pre-war" style clothes. Mrs Renouard was a dental assistant. She was born in Alsace, a French department bordering Germany. She spoke with the regional accent. Her hus-

*Josette, Mrs Renouard, Rachel, Maman Suzanne, Leon, Papa Henri*

band was a painter at the Renault factory in Paris. Both were very kind people. Mrs Renouard's sister, Blanche, her pretty 20-year-old daughter, Josette, and sometimes Mrs Renouard's brother, Lucien, would join them. We were always so happy to see them. They brought a Parisian atmosphere. It was a wonderful diversion from the grey life we endured. They would always bring presents, which we could never find in our little town of Compiègne. They seemed to come from another planet. To us Paris was the center of the universe. The capital of France seemed so far away at that time and very special.

Many people who lived outside of Paris had an inferiority complex toward the Parisians. When Paris was mentioned, we thought of our parents. Drancy, the town where our parents had been taken after their arrest was a suburb of Paris. *Could they still be there, so close to us?*

Josette was a princess to me. I loved to watch her when she was not looking in my direction. She was so beautiful, so elegant. She often wore a light-colored suit with a matching skirt, gloves and carried a fashionable handbag. I think that Marcel was in love with her. But he was probably intimidated by her beauty, elegance, and Parisian confidence. He never dated her, to the chagrin of the families.

From the few comments I recall, Papa and Maman Ribouleau would have liked her as their daughter-in-law.

We got together quite often with the Mouton family. They lived in Compiègne. George Mouton was Maman Suzanne's brother. His wife, Lucie, was a nurse at the hospital where I was born. My son Olivier was born twenty-five years later at the same hospital. George and Lucie had three daughters. Their eldest, a pretty girl named Georgette had contracted polio when she was young. The illness left her with a deformed spinal column. The other two, Lucette and Jacqueline were respectively about the same age as Rachel and I. We all got along well. They lived around the corner from us on "rue de Paris." I often played with Jacqueline at their house, the same house where we saw the prisoners coming to the detention camp and coming from the detention camp to the train station on their way to the extermination camps.

Maman Suzanne's sister, Aunt Marie Germain, also lived in Compiègne. We rarely saw her. She was a domineering person. Whenever we were around her, Rachel and I kept quiet since we were afraid that she would reprimand us for no reason. Her husband André was highly intelligent, yet, very timid and unassuming. He stuttered, and many blamed his wife for his condition. Their daughter, Jeanine, was also very much afraid of her mother. She was very kind to Rachel and me.

When we had guests, Maman Suzanne was always concerned about having enough food for all. Most of the time, we ate a rabbit or a chicken from our henhouse along with vegetables from our gardens. There was always a homemade pie for dessert made with fruits from the garden. I loved these visits, the conversations, the card games, the fishing trips. For a few hours or a day or two, we tried to forget the stress of the dreadful life we lived day after day under the yoke of the German occupation.

There were very few distractions.

On Saturdays, however, Marcel Ribouleau went to a dance hall called Pinson. Local musicians—mainly accordionists and pianists— performed there. It was about the only entertainment in town on weekends, except for the two movie theaters to which we never went, as it was too expensive and played mostly propaganda movies.

At that time, René was dating his future wife, Cécile, a gentle and intelligent person. They planned to get married after the liberation. The wedding took place on October 27, 1945 a few months after France regained its freedom. After working in a bank for two years, René began a career at the SNCF (Société Nationale des Chemins de Fer) National Railroad, in 1943.

I don't remember ever celebrating my birthday during the gloomy Occupation years. Christmas was the time I always looked forward to impatiently. Papa and Maman Ribouleau were non-practicing Catholics, like most French people. I never knew whether they believed in God or not. A crucifix hung above their beds. They went to church only for baptisms, weddings, and funerals. Papa Henri was uncomfortable when he went to church on these occasions. He did not care for organized religion.

I liked going with Maman Suzanne to the Christmas midnight mass at the small Saint-Germain church. The inside was decorated and brightly lit with many candles. Being there was an entertainment and a change from the gloomy evenings we spent in the dark of winter. Toward the end of the war, to avoid being seen by the Allied air raids, we were not allowed to have any light on after sunset.

When Mrs Renouard and her husband visited us during the Christmas holidays, she came with us to the midnight mass. Her husband, also named Henri, hated anything that had to do with religion. I liked listening to the organ music and the Christmas songs sung by a choir, though I did not know any of them.

Toward the end of the Mass most people stood up and walked to the priest to receive communion. I felt uneasy and always remained seated except once. To avoid drawing attention to myself, I decided to follow everyone else. I remember feeling very uncomfortable as I followed the line. I had no idea what communion was. I felt that I was doing something forbidden. I did not understand why. I wanted so much to be like everybody else. The priest gave me no special attention when he placed the host on my tongue while my eyes were shut. I returned to my seat, somewhat confused and feeling guilty.

Our Christian family never tried to convert us. Religion was never an issue in the family and was never brought up.

Rachel and I were afraid of the word "Jew." We couldn't stand hearing the word. Bad news was associated with this word. It reminded us of our parents' arrest and the constant danger we were exposed to. I erased the word "Jew" from my vocabulary for many years during and long after the war ended.

After the midnight mass, we would assemble in the dining room and celebrate "le Réveillon," Christmas Eve. Each year, Papa Henri brought home a small pine tree from the nearby forest. We decorated it with pieces of yarn of different colors and cotton balls to simulate snow. Cotton was also laid in front of the fireplace in the living room.

Maman Suzanne pulled out her prettiest embroidered table-cloth to cover the dining room table. I did not expect toys, as there were none available. Toy factories had been converted to the man-ufacturing of war-related commodities. I always hoped that Santa would bring me a surprise. I was a strong believer in Santa.

One Christmas morning when I was six or seven years old, I found an orange hidden in the cotton. What an extraordinary gift! It was the first time that I saw an orange. I lifted it very gently as I would a delicate object, afraid to drop it. I turned it around and around many times before smelling its subtle and unusual smell. I had no idea where they were grown, but I knew somehow that or-anges came from a place with sun and blue skies. As I closed my eyes I was transported to a faraway, colorful and exotic country.

Did oranges grow on a tree like peaches and cherries or in the ground like potatoes and carrots?

I had no doubt that Santa Claus had brought it down the chim-ney just for me. The orange was so fragrant and its skin texture and color so striking, that I couldn't resolve myself to eat it. I looked at it every day for what seemed a long time. I kept my precious orange in a drawer. Eventually, it shriveled up, became hard and inedible. I was upset but happy nevertheless to have received such an unusual gift and kept it without destroying it. Some other Christmas, I re-ceived a sweater or a scarf knitted by Maman Suzanne or Rachel, as well as books from our friends, the Renouards.

When Papa Henri had a few hours, he would take me fishing by the river. There were very few commercial boats in those days. The water was quiet most of the time. It was a wonderful feeling to come home with many small silver fish we would fry and eat from head to tail. They were delicious. For bait, we used fresh bread that we rolled into a very small ball. It wasn't easy to keep these mushy bread balls on the fishhook. We also used maggots that we bred by keeping meat in sawdust in a small can pierced with holes large enough for flies to go in and lay their eggs.

We sometimes positioned ourselves next to a pipe that brought the animal blood from the slaughterhouse into the river. Cows, horses, sheep and pigs were killed there for the local butchers. Blood from the dead animals ran directly into the river then. It attracted fish, and at the same time it was polluting this beautiful river. A German soldier, in civilian clothes, often came to fish there. He spoke to Papa Henri in fairly good French. One time he asked Papa for his name. They would exchange small talk.

Now and then during the summer, we would go to the lakes Saint Pierre on Sundays, about ten miles from our home. It was an expedition! Maman Suzanne prepared a picnic. Papa Henri towed a small two-wheel trailer behind his bike. Rachel and I sat in it, surrounded by the food and the fishing equipment. Papa Henri had strong legs. He needed them to pull this very heavy load with a bicycle without a derailleur. As a young man, he was a competitive runner. Maman Suzanne rode her bike with us. René and Marcel would borrow bikes from their friends or neighbors to accompany us.

We would leave very early to make sure we would have a good spot. We hoped that we wouldn't get a flat tire on the way and that it would not rain. We set up our blanket and the necessities for the picnic next to the lake.

Before lunch when the weather was good, we went swimming in the area reserved for that purpose. In those days, it was believed that you had to wait three hours after eating before going in the water. The water was cold and not very clear. I didn't know how to swim, but we still had fun jumping around, screaming and splashing each other.

After lunch, we would resume fishing. For lake fishing we used maggots and earthworms for bait, which we found in the garden or in the manure heap at the back of the garden. To attract the fish to the spot we had set up, Papa Henri prepared a "secret" recipe mix which he later shared with me. He used bran flour to which he added a few drops of Pastis or Pernod alcohol leftover from before the war. The mix was rolled into balls two to three inches in diameter, which we threw with precision at the spot where our floaters were.

The ladies sat close to us, knitting and talking.

The fish we caught were kept in the water in a wire mesh basket attached to a wooden stake stuck on the bank. One evening, the basket was filled to the brim with a miraculous catch. As we were getting ready to go home, I was playing with the basket admiring this exceptional bounty, I accidentally dropped it in the water and to my horror, it quickly sunk to the bottom of the lake. The sun was already low, behind the tall trees, and we couldn't see the basket with the fish inside.

"Léon, why did you have to play with the basket full of fish?" scolded Papa Henri.

I didn't know what to say. I was so embarrassed by what I had done. I disappointed everyone. I wanted to get lost in the woods surrounding the lake.

"It's time to leave. You come back tomorrow morning. You may be able to see it and you will be able to pick it up. Let's go," said Maman Suzanne.

During the whole trip back I hid my face, overcome with shame. I had spoiled a great day and lost a superb catch. *What will we eat tonight?*

We got up very early the next morning. It was a bright sunny day. At 6:00 a.m., we were back at our fishing place. Oh happiness! We could see the fish moving inside the basket at the bottom of the lake. Papa Henri, using a leaded fishing line and a large hook, quickly recovered the basket, intact. I was so happy and relieved. All the fish were still alive.

Each of these outings put the worries of the war on hold for a few hours.

Chapter 11

# Constant Fear

Miraculously, we survived and overcame the many dangerous obstacles for almost three years.

The Germans, with the collaboration of the French authorities, knew where we were living. We no longer had the possibility to escape from the town. *Where could we have gone anyway? Who would want to take care of us?*

The French police had arrested our parents at the same address where we continued to live during the entire German occupation. My sister was almost ten years old at the time of our parent's deportation and, according to the law of those days she should have been wearing the star of David. She never did. Neither did I. *How did we get away with it?* We were hidden in plain sight. We continued to go to school, play in the street with the neighborhood children and go to the grocery store or the farm daily to get our milk.

Everyone around us was aware of our situation. We never changed our names. The town was swarming with German soldiers and SS. We were at the mercy of a denunciation by our neighbors, our teachers, the employees of the town hall and collaborators. We lived with fear and stress twenty-four hours a day. Some neighbors continued to express their concern to Papa Henri and Maman Suzanne:

"Why are you keeping these children? You are risking your life and your children's lives. You may be deported and even shot for hiding Jews. They will find them anyway."

They, in not so many words, were strongly encouraging Papa and Maman Ribouleau to turn us over to the Gestapo.

And Papa Henri and Maman Suzanne continued to respond:

"We promised Monsieur and Madame Malmed that we would take care of the children until they returned. These children are not hurting anyone. They need us. We will protect them."

71

Their answer stood firm until the liberation. Protecting us at the risk of their lives was natural to them. They were conscious of the dangers of their actions, but handing us over to the Germans or to the French police would have been like giving their own sons away. Did they, at times, doubt the merits of their decision? I do not think so.

René and Marcel, who were now young adults, were aware of the dangers as well, but nonetheless they always treated us like their brother and sister. They never showed any jealousy or animosity toward us, although we took away scarce food from them and forced them to live in fear as well.

The Clausse family, our first-floor neighbors, never shared the concern of some other neighbors. On the contrary, they were affectionate with us and supportive of the Ribouleaus.

Among the neighbors who were very concerned with our presence was a couple living next door to us. The husband was a mail carrier. I remember his mustache "à la Hitler" that gave him a fixed ironic smile. Whenever we saw him, he would smile and we would respectfully say: "Bonjour monsieur." His wife harbored a severe red face at all times. We were much afraid of her. She never smiled. She seemed angry all the time. She often questioned our presence with Papa Henri and Maman Suzanne.

One day, in a bind, Maman Suzanne asked her if she could watch us for half an hour. She categorically refused. We were very concerned that she would denounce us. Apparently she never did, despite her unfriendly behavior. Fortunately, many other neighbors were sympathetic.

The Bataille family lived a few houses down the street. They had two sons, Paul and Jacques. Jacques was a few years older than I. He accompanied me to school. Their father was a World War I veteran. He suffered from lung problems due to the damages caused by the chemical weapons that were used during that war. He died in 1944, less than a year before the liberation of our town. Paul Bataille told me many years later that their father had instructed his family never to talk about my sister and me outside of their home to avoid creating problems for us.

Twice a year, the school gave each pupil a number of "anti-tuberculosis" stamps, designed to collect funds for medical research to fight the disease, which in those days killed thousands of people a year. Madame Bataille was one of the few who welcomed me with a smile and bought many of my stamps. I was eager to sell all the stamps I had been given. The teachers were not happy if we brought any back. I was proud to participate in this fund-raising for such a good cause. After selling the stamps, I would jingle the coins in my pocket, anticipating the smile on my teacher's face when I would tell him that I sold them all.

The Savouret family lived a few houses up the street. Monsieur and Madame Savouret sold flowers in the town square. Madame Savouret spoke with a very unique "bee-like" accent, typical of the small town where she was born. All the residents of that village, located about ten miles from Compiègne, spoke that way. We trusted that family.

My sister was often invited to play at the home of Micheline Vallée. Her father's radio repair shop was attached to their house. While working, he wore a white smock and looked to me like a radio doctor. There were no TVs back then.

During the occupation, Jews were forbidden to own a radio. Everyone else could, but no one was allowed to listen to Radio London under the penalty of arrests, deportation or death. Most people did. Radio London broadcast every evening. We made sure that the sound could not be heard outside of the room where the radio was located.

At one time, Monsieur Vallée was arrested and brought to the SS headquarters for interrogation. An unhappy customer or a jealous neighbor probably denounced him. Very few people ever came out of that building to go home. He did, much to the relief of his family and everyone in the neighborhood. So many people depended on his skill to keep the fragile radio, called "TSF" (wireless), working.

At the corner of the main road rue de Paris and the rue Saint-Fiacre was the butcher, Monsieur Legrand. His home and shop were attached. I remember his round red face. It was unusual to see anyone with rosy cheeks in those days. Most people lived on less than one thousand calories a day. Meat was rare, almost nonexistent. As a butcher, Monsieur Legrand was able to keep his family fed. That family also took serious risks by hiding a Jewish child during the war.

The Coppée family lived across the street from us. Monsieur Coppée worked for the Post Office, which was then responsible for the mail, telephone, and telegraph. Their daughter, Ginette, went to the same school and was in the same class as Rachel. Monsieur and Madame Coppée were very reserved and rarely engaged with their neighbors. We trusted them, as well.

Our freedom, and now we know, our lives, depended on all of these people. One word to the wrong person, and we would have lost both our freedom and our lives. We often wondered who could be capable of denouncing us. Were all the people who knew about us hiding in plain sight our friends? Would someone trade us for some favors? Would they give us away for an extra food ration card? Getting food was a round the clock worry. The gardens helped in summertime only. It was impossible to get food without connections or something of value to trade. We continued to live with the ever-present fear that anyone who knew about us and many did, including our teachers, our school mates, our street neighbors would talk to someone who was friendly with the Germans or go to the Germans directly. *Who was a friend, who was a collaborator? How could we tell if the smile we saw did not conceal some darker thoughts?* We were never at peace.

Rachel and I were also concerned that Papa Henri and Maman Suzanne would grow tired of carrying such a heavy burden. Despite all the pressure, they kept their promise to our parents and shielded us against the rumors, the fear, the hunger, the arrest, and the possibility of being shot.

Almost across the street from us, a woman dated a German officer. A low-ranking soldier drove him in a sidecar to her apartment several times a week. Although she would always smile at us when we saw each other in the street, we were very afraid that she would tell her lover about the neighbors hiding two Jewish children.

The day of the liberation of our town, the Underground fighters arrested her, along with all the other women who fraternized with the enemy. Their hair was shaved. They were forced to climb into a horse-drawn carriage that was otherwise used to carry manure or refuse and paraded across town for several hours while people booed as they passed. Some of them went to jail. We never saw nor heard of our neighbor again. She did not denounce us as far as we know, or her lover chose to remain silent.

Living in constant fear the way we did, we were easily startled by any unusual noise. German army motorized vehicles were the only vehicles in the streets. Long after after our parents had been taken away, I woke up screaming around five o'clock in the morning—that fateful hour when the gendarmes had arrested our parents—convinced that my turn had come. I could not see a uniform in the streets without being terrorized. Still, we had to act normally, and face some unpleasant and sometimes hostile looks. I went to school. Papa Henri and Maman Suzanne went to work between the alerts. We kept hoping that the Allies would soon liberate us and that our parents would be back. We desperately wanted the nightmare to end, for our lives to return to normal and be together again, living happy lives without fearing what could happen the next minute, the next hour, the next day.

Victory seemed distant and uncertain. Despite it all, we went on living in a world that was upside down. I played in the street with the neighborhood children. Every evening, the family assembled around the radio, with the sound level on very low. Radio London gave us the latest news on the war and words of encouragement from General de Gaulle.* His optimism gave us hope that the Allied Forces were making progress and would win the war. Liberation was soon to come, he said.

Such a day was a dream that seemed so close at times but realistically far away.

Papa Henri and Maman Suzanne were on high alert all the time. All kinds of rumors circulated regularly. They were very vigilant. Whenever they heard of a potential roundup, they would take us out of school and keep us hidden, sometimes for several days. We stood ready to escape through the fields behind our garden. We had no idea where we would go from there. No one we knew wanted us. At such times, the hours seemed very long. We hardly moved or talked. We never approached the windows for fear that someone would see us. We held our breath when we heard a motor noise. Our street was normally quiet. We hoped that the gendarmes or the soldiers would not come for us.

Sometimes, we would hide in one of the cellars. There were three of them, one for each apartment. The smell of coal and potatoes, both very rare, was strong. A single light bulb was hanging from the ceiling. It was turned off for fear of giving us away. It was dark and

---

* Charles de Gaulle (1890–1970) was the highest-ranking French officer who did not accept the German armistice. He escaped to London, from where he organized the Free French forces and made radio broadcasts to the French Underground and the French population.

humid. Papa Henri had built a wood structure to support the ceiling in case a bomb hit our building directly. Only two small people like my sister and me could fit there. In winter, we would wrap ourselves in a blanket to fight the cold. At times, we would stay there for hours. I would close my eyes. That was unnecessary since no daylight filtered in the cellar. It was easier not to see the rats, the mice and the monsters that surely lived there.

When I tried to talk, Rachel silenced me with a "shhh." I would feel her hand on my shoulder, and I was reassured instantly.

The wait was unbearable in this dark, humid, and cold place. I stood silently counting or reciting a few poems that I learned in school. I thought of my kites. I wished I was one of them and could fly far away from this city, carried away by the wind. Maybe I would have flown over land and oceans to the labor camp where I was told my parents might be held captive. They were a tailor and a seamstress. For sure, they were working in a clothing factory over there. I could help them. Perhaps, they could hold on to my kite and escape from their prison to follow me to a country where we all would be free, happy and together at last, the Malmed and the Ribouleau families.

When the alert was over, Papa Henri would come and get us out of this dark hole. First we would hear the door of the basement open. Papa Henri would turn on the light. He would call us from the top of the stairs to reassure us.

"Leon! Rachel! It's me, everything is O.K. The alert is over. Come out," he would say joyfully.

I would let my kite escape in the sky full of dark threatening clouds and open my eyes. Papa Henri would welcome us with open arms. We would rush there and take comfort in his embrace.

"Everything is okay. Are you hungry?" Papa Henri asked.

We would climb the stairs to the ground level and then to the first floor, staggering a bit for having stayed for hours barely moving, blinded by the daylight. Maman Suzanne would greet us with a big smile. She would hold out a piece of bread or a fruit, usually an apple from the garden when they were available. We sat on our chairs, chewing the food slowly, savoring every bite.

We belonged to the world of the living again.

That was our life until the end of the war.

# Chapter 12

# Royallieu

The internment and deportation Camp of Royallieu was located a quarter mile from the rue Saint-Fiacre where we lived. The only entrance and exit was on the main thoroughfare rue de Paris with rue du Mouton on the north side, and rue Saint Germain on the backside. This detention camp was renamed by the Germans during the war, Frontstalag 122.

Built in 1913 on thirty-seven acres, it served as a French military hospital for many years. In June 1940, the Germans took over the camp and converted it to army barracks. Within a few months the German troops were moved to another location and the camp became an internment camp for French and British prisoners. Frontstalag 122 was run exclusively by the German army, the Sicherheitsdienst. It soon became a major internment camp for political prisoners, resistance fighters, and other captured foreign nationals such as the British, Russians, Italians, antifascists and others who were deemed dangerous by the Nazis or fell under the German racial laws.* About ten percent of the camp detainees were Jews. They were held in an area called camp C. The conditions of camp C were similar to those of the extermination camps: starvation, non-existent hygienic conditions, and no medical care. During the terribly cold winter of 1941–1942, there was no heat, and hardly any water or food. Many of the Jewish detainees died before deportation. Starting in 1942, all Jews arrested were sent directly to Drancy.

Between March 1942 and August 1944, around 54,000 men and women were interned in Frontstalag 122 for days, weeks, or months. Over the course of the war about 50,000 of them were deported to the concentration and extermination camps whose

---

* The Nuremberg Race Laws of 1935 deprived German Jews of their rights of citizenship, giving them the status of "subjects" in Hitler's Reich. The laws also made it illegal for Jews to marry or have sexual relations with ethnic Germans or to employ German women under 45 in Jewish households.

names resonate in our memories in a sinister way: Auschwitz, Ravensbrück, Buchenwald, Flossenburg, Dachau, Sachsenhausen, Mauthausen, and Neuengamme. Fifty-four convoys left from the Compiègne railroad station with an average of a thousand per convoy and one hundred people per sealed cattle car, 28 × 8.5 feet, or 2.7 sq.ft. per person.

In school, a number of Rachel's schoolmates had distanced themselves from her as if she had contracted a contagious disease. I guess they were concerned about being associated with a Jewish girl. My sister's best friend Marie Lesueur lived on rue du Mouton, one of the streets that surrounded the camp. Marie was kind and gentle and showed much affection for my sister. It helped Rachel cope with the difficult conditions.

Most of the twenty or so houses across the street from the camp had a second floor from which you could see inside the camp. The owners of these houses would let family members of the internees go to the upstairs rooms where they would try to connect with their relatives by screaming their names. In many cases, they did not know if their loved ones were even inside the camp. The Red Cross had limited success in getting the names of the internees at any of the more than fifty detention camps in France. When they did get information, they would contact the families of the internees and advise them as to the location of their relatives. The families would come to Compiègne, in some cases from faraway towns requiring a day or two of travel, with hopes of seeing and communicating with their relatives.

The internees came from everywhere in France as well as from other countries. They were communists, priests, wealthy, poor, and all innocent of a crime. Many had been denounced on trumped-up charges by personal enmity. Some were accused of black marketeering, a necessity to survive. Among the internees were many intellectuals like the poet Robert Desnos.*

Whenever a Germans soldier was killed or wounded by the Underground, the Germans picked a number of prisoners, 40 to 1, at random from the civilian hostage pool and shot them.

---

* The French poet Robert Desnos was born July 4, 1900, in Paris. He was arrested in 1944 by the Gestapo as a member of the Resistance and died of typhoid on June 8, 1945 in the Terezin, Czechoslovakia concentration camp shortly after its liberation. His books *Waking* (1943) and *Country* (1944) are among the most powerful monuments of the tragic and heroic poetry of that time.

The Germans quickly put an end to the only way families could communicate with the internees by banning the use of the upstairs rooms of all the homes with a second floor surrounding Frontstalag 122.

My sister and Marie started to use a subterfuge. They pretended that they were playing in the street while they were shouting names of internees that families had provided them. Occasionally, someone would be heard and a message would be delivered either vocally or by way of a ball of paper thrown over the fence. The contractors who delivered food and services often put their lives in danger by passing on messages as well.

In front of the camp, on Rue de Paris, the Germans had installed substantial barriers in a serpentine pattern to prevent any vehicles from exceeding five miles per hour. A twelve-foot wooden fence surrounded the camp to make it impossible to see inside from the street. In addition to the perimeter fence was a triple network of barbed wires. Day and night, the soldiers in the watchtowers, equipped with powerful spotlights and machine-guns, made escaping about impossible. The sidewalks bordering the camp were forbidden to civilians. Signs read, "Any person approaching the fence will be shot." Despite all that, there were a number of escape attempts, and one hundred detainees managed to gain freedom, mostly through tunnels, over the course of the war.

Like most children at that age, Rachel and her friend Marie were curious. They had been told many times not to walk on the sidewalk next to the camp and certainly not to come close to the fence which was about thirty feet across the street from the front door of Marie's home. One time, unable to resist their curiosity, they crossed the street and peeked through a small hole in the fence. Perhaps Rachel had hoped for a miracle and see our parents. They saw many barracks lined up around a courtyard where people milled around. A German soldier came from the street waving his rifle at them and screaming, scaring them away. They did not tell anyone about that event for a long time.

The French internees were separated from the English, Russians, Belgians, and other foreign internees, and were not allowed to communicate with the other groups. Most of the detainees in Frontstalag 122 had been tortured when they were arrested. They knew nothing about their future. The dismal conditions of this camp were still better than what they had experienced in the French jails at the hands of the Nazi SS. None of them knew how long they would stay in this camp nor did they know where the ones leaving were going.

They thought that they were being sent to work camps in Germany or other occupied countries. While awaiting departure some played cards, soccer with improvised balls, or any other games to keep busy. Others put together theater presentations, organized non-political and non-war-related conferences. Life in the camp was precarious. There was very little food, no medical supply, unhygienic conditions and vermin infested beds. There was practically no heat in winter in the barracks. Any activity helped to hold on to hope and sanity. Keeping busy was the only way to uphold the morale of men and women who did not have the slightest notion of what the next day, next week, next month would bring. They had no news from the outside and no idea who was winning the war. Had they known what was awaiting them at the end of the journey, many more would have attempted to escape and many more rebellions would have taken place.

Similarly to the procedure in Drancy, the night before departures to the unknown destination, the internees on the list were placed in an empty building. During the night, prayers, songs and sobbing could be heard. Some had hopes for better conditions. Many wrote messages that would be thrown in the streets or from the train hoping that someone would find it and mail it to their family. Many of these messages did reach their destinations. Deportees did not know that they would be traveling in sealed cattle cars where one hundred of them would be shoved in. Many of them would die during the next three to five days from thirst, suffocation, heat exhaustion or being trampled.

Sometimes, family members informed by the Red Cross of the departure of their loved ones would come to Compiègne to try to contact or just catch a glimpse of their relative as they walked from the camp to the railroad station. The one thousand deportees traveled the four-mile trip on foot surrounded by German soldiers with their ferocious German shepherds and French gendarmes. Some deportees carried a suitcase or a bag, some a blanket, the typical loaf of bread, often moldy, and a sausage given to each of them the night before. The deportees were herded from the camp to the railroad station very early in the morning to avoid being seen by too many citizens. The Germans had passed an ordinance ordering all houses located on the streets used by the deportees to and from the railroad station to keep windows and shutters closed when convoys were passing by. It was enforced by soldiers on motorcycles riding ahead of the convoys.

There were few pedestrians at that time of the morning. There were always a few courageous ones who tried and sometimes succeeded in handing the deportees some bread and food and to yell "Courage." Some bystanders looked at the ground or looked away either scared of being hurt or overwhelmed by pity.

When we were at Uncle Mouton's home, we peeked through the closed shutters. I saw many of these poor human beings departing. We did not know that they were marching to their death or slavery. Many of them were singing the French anthem: "La Marseillaise," or Beethoven's "Hymne à la Joie," "Hymn to Happiness" to give themselves courage. Families of the deportees who came hoping that they would be able to see, hug, and kiss their loved ones were crying and blowing kisses. The SS and the French police and their dogs kept them at a distance.

The train with its ten cattle cars was waiting at the station for the trip to hell. For the next three to five days they would try to stay alive in the cramped space with no room to sit, with one bucket of water and one bucket for waste per car. The minuscule window did not provide enough air for all of them to breathe. On the station platforms, many soldiers with automatic rifles and dogs prevented the outraged French railroad workers and anyone else from coming close to the train.

No one besides the Germans knew the destination of these convoys. Before leaving, the deportees filled out a card to be mailed to their family on which they were told to write: "I am being transferred to another camp. Do not send any packages. Wait for my new address."

Once in the camp, if they survived the selections, a very few deportees were authorized to send a card or a strictly controlled letter to their family. This would give renewed hope to many other families and perpetuate the delusion they were okay—"là-bas"—over

there. The deportees arriving in Auschwitz-Birkenau or other extermination camps were greeted by the savage SS soldiers and their
dogs, disappearing in the dark and foggy nights of the extermination camps.

The poor souls who passed by our windows on their way to the
man-made hells of the Reich already looked wasted due to lack of
food and proper hygiene while they stayed in Royallieu and French
prison, prior to their arrival at the detention camp. No one could
imagine the horror they were destined to endure if they were still
alive after the transport and the first selection. No one could imagine the barbaric treatment that only a very few would survive to tell.

Today, more than sixty years later, despite compelling evidence,
thousands of witnesses, testimonies and confessions, some still re-
fute that the Holocaust ever took place.

During the war, before falling asleep, I would think of the day
my parents would come back from this "là-bas," a place where the
soldiers dressed in black or ugly green uniforms might take my sister and me. It is at this "là-bas" that all the people marching from
Frontstalag 122 to the train station would join Papa and Maman.

# Chapter 13

# The Roundup

Wednesday, January 19, 1944. They came to arrest us, my sister and me. I am six years old and Rachel eleven.

I was home with a cold that day. Papa Henri missed work to stay with me. Rachel was in school. Maman Suzanne was coming home for lunch on her bicycle, as she did every day. For some reason, she chose to take a different route that day. As she was passing by the home of the Baugis family where my cousin Charlot was hidden since his parents' arrest on July 19, 1942, she saw the infamous black truck with several SS soldiers and some men wearing the militia uniform, long leather coats and black hats in front of the house. She suddenly had the foreboding feeling that their next stop would be 17 rue St Fiacre. She pedaled as fast as she could.

About five minutes later, she was climbing the stairs two by two to our apartment, out of breath, screaming:

"They are coming, quick, quick, go and hide, go and hide."

Papa Henri and I rushed down the stairs, went to the neighbor's house. They were the same people who had refused to keep us once before. There was no time to go elsewhere. He knocked on the door. They opened the door, just slightly. Papa Henri quickly explained the situation and asked if they could keep me for a little while.

They refused and said, with the door closing: "Do not insist. We do not want any problems because of these children. We already told you that."

We came back to the courtyard of our building. Papa Henri, desperate, was looking at the stone wall at the end of the garden and said suddenly:

"Hurry, Leon, jump over the wall. Run through the field toward rue Saint Germain. I will meet you there with my bicycle. If you do not see me, go to Tante Beauchard. Do not turn back. Do not speak to anyone. Do not look afraid. Do you understand?

"Oui, oui Papa, j'ai compris,"—"Yes, yes, papa, I understand," I answered.

"Run, run, run," Papa Henri said.

He helped me over the heap of manure resting against the wall and the chicken coop. I fell on the other side and ran the half-mile as fast as I could, across the wheat field, which was bare at that time of the year. As I started to run, I heard the motor noise of the hated truck as well as the horrible guttural speaking of the SS soldiers. Papa was already waiting for me on the other side of the field. I wiped off my hands that were full of manure and mud on my pants before sitting on the frame of his bicycle. We quickly covered the four to five miles to Aunt Beauchard. She was Papa Henri's sister-in-law, the wife of his half-brother who had died of cancer a few years before the war. Aunt Beauchard was a frail person of about sixty who rarely smiled. She had yellowish skin with one or two clusters of beard on her chin. We did not like to kiss her, mainly for that reason. She always dressed in gray or black. Whenever we saw each other, which was infrequently, she looked at us suspiciously. She never showed any affection toward us. She could not understand why her brother-in-law and his wife would be taking such risks for children who were total strangers to the family.

It was a rainy day. We arrived drenched. We crossed the large courtyard and climbed the stairs to the third-floor apartment. Papa Henri knocked. She opened the door but did not invite us in. He explained the situation and asked if we could stay for a few days. I kept looking at the floor afraid to offend her. Very reluctantly, she let us come into her one-room apartment.

"It is only for a few days," repeated Papa Henri.

"Hiding these children, are you crazy? Suzanne and you are not thinking straight," Aunt Beauchard shouted.

In the meantime, Maman Suzanne had gone back, still on her bicycle, toward Rachel's school, hoping to intercept her before she got home for lunchtime. She caught up with her a quarter of a mile from our home. She saw the SS truck turning the corner of our street.

Maman Suzanne and Rachel joined us at Aunt Beauchard's home, who by now was trembling with anger and fear.

Papa Henri took Maman Suzanne outside of the apartment and told her of the dire situation. Rachel and I were sitting quietly. Rachel was close to me as Aunt Beauchard stared at us, repeating:

"No, I cannot keep them. It is too dangerous."

Maman Suzanne decided not to go back to work that afternoon. Around 4 p.m., Papa, anxious to find out what was happening at rue St Fiacre, and to make sure that the SS did not leave a watch by our building, rode his bike toward our apartment. He stopped at the bottom of our street and saw that the SS truck was still in front of our home and to his horror, he saw his son René being pushed inside the truck! Paralyzed by fear for René, he stood there with probably a thousand thoughts going through his mind. He could have gone to the German soldiers and offered us in exchange for his son. He did not.

The truck did not move for a long time. It seemed that they were waiting for our return or trying to get some information from our neighbors on our whereabouts. After what seemed to Papa, hours, he told us afterwards, he saw René coming out of the truck, taking his bicycle and pedaling toward the bottom of the street where Papa Henri stood, not knowing that his father was there.

René had learned that Rachel and I were to be arrested early that morning but for a miraculous reason, there was a smudge over our address that made it unreadable. The SS decided to go to the next address and come back later. They came back at lunchtime but we were not there. They missed us by minutes. As René was coming home for lunch, as he turned the corner of our street he saw the truck in front of our building. It was the major roundup we had feared so he decided not to stop. The SS soldiers, probably angry not to have found us, stopped him as he was passing by. They asked him if he knew the Malmed children. "Never heard the name," he told them. They told him to get in the truck without asking for his I.D.

There were a number of people in the truck he knew and who knew him. No one said a word. It was a miracle that the SS did not ask to see René's identity papers. Had they done that, they would have known that he was lying and brought him to the SS headquarters for interrogation to be followed by deportation or worse. The name Ribouleau was associated with the name Malmed. Maybe the SS were in a hurry to get back to lunch! They let him go. He came so close to torture and death.

The truck was still in front of the building as Papa Henri, af-

ter being reassured that René was safe, decided to come back to
Tante Beauchard's apartment. She stood by the door with her arms
crossed against her chest and spat out:

"I do not want you and them to stay here another minute. You
lost your mind. You must give the children to the Germans. Leave
now or I report you."

She was livid. She was so scared, even more scared than us.

Rachel and I were very frightened by her screaming. The neighbors could hear her, we were sure.

Night was falling. We expected the soldiers to be waiting for us
at home.

It was almost curfew time. A decision had to be made. Tante
Beauchard did not want us to stay. We had nowhere else to go. It
was January. It was too cold to spend the night outdoors.

"Let's go home," said Papa Henri.

There was no other solution. We followed him out. He con-
tained his anger and deep disappointment. We all walked back
home pushing the bicycles and not uttering a word. We knew that
they were waiting for us.

No soldier was in front of our building or in the hallway. We
slowly climbed the stairs waiting to hear a "Halt!" command any
second. Nothing. We went inside. René and Marcel were waiting
for us. They said that the SS did not come back and did not leave a
sentry.

We went to bed with our clothes on, convinced that the SS
would come back in the middle of the night or early in the morning. No one slept that night, jumping at the faintest noise.

We did not go to school the following week. We stayed home,
shut out from the world in the dining room or in the cellar waiting
for the horrible SS soldiers who surely would arrive at any moment
barking orders. At any motor noise in the street, we became paralyzed. I would nestle close to my sister. She would reassure me, as
she did so many times.

*How could we escape this impossible situation? Who would take
the risk of helping us Jewish children?*

No one outside of this family wanted us. We did not have any
identity papers. The only public transportation was the railroad. All
the train stations were being watched. Every person boarding a train
was asked to show his I.D. Where would we go anyway?

Remembering that our parents hardly had time to pack when the gendarmes came to arrest them, Maman Suzanne had prepared a pack for each of us with warm clothes, two pairs of shoes, soap and food in case the SS came back.

After a few days, not able to control his anxiety, Papa Henri went to the SS headquarters and asked to speak to the German soldier Hoffmann, whom he had met while fishing a number of times.

Hoffman had given his name to Papa Henri and had told him to come and see him if he had any problems. He had only seen this German soldier in civilian clothes. He had no idea of his rank, but due to his demeanor guessed that he was an officer. A few minutes later, Papa discovered that Hoffman was the commander of the German headquarters, the Kommandantur, in Compiègne. We never knew if he was part of the SS or the Wehrmacht.*

Apparently, he was aware that the Ribouleau family was hiding us. When Papa Henri explained the reason he came to see him, Hoffman told him:

"Do not worry. No harm will come to your family and to the children. From here on, they are in no danger as long as I am here."

Papa Henri felt an enormous weight lifting off his shoulders. He was dumbfounded, seeing this man whom he had only seen in civilian clothes, who appeared to be a civilized person, who enjoyed fishing like him, behind an impressive desk in a German uniform and in such an important position.

We went back to school and resumed our daily life. Papa Henri and Maman Suzanne returned to work.

Why did this man protect us? We will never know.

A few weeks later, a well-dressed woman wearing lots of jewelry came to our home. She explained to Papa Henri that she was responsible for protecting hidden Jewish children. She wanted to take us to a more secure place until the end of the war. Papa Henri did not like her and quickly became suspicious of her. She did not say how she knew of us. He refused her offer categorically. He remembered the promise he had made to our parents on July 19, 1942.

She was very upset.

"You are wrong," she said. "These children are not safe with you. The SS will find them easily."

---

* The Wehrmacht was the regular armed forces of Germany, as opposed to the Waffen SS, the military branch of the Nazi Party.

"Please, do not insist," said Papa Henri. He almost threw her out.

We never heard of her again and we never knew who she was or for whom she was working.

Years later, in 1953, Josette and Lucien Zinc, friends from Paris, had decided to go and visit the castle of Compiègne.* It was 4:45 p.m. As they came to the entrance of the castle, the attendant told them that the visits ended at 4:30 p.m. They would have to come back the next day. As they were leaving, disappointed, the attendant let a couple speaking German into the castle.

Lucien, who spoke fluent German, went back to the custodian and asked, "Why do you let them in and not us?"

"He is Mr Hoffman, the ex-commander of the Kommandantur of Compiègne," he said, lifting his arms in the air as if to say "How could you not know who this man was. Isn't it obvious?"

Lucien, shocked by the event, told Papa Henri about it. He had no idea that Papa knew this person. This man may have saved the lives of my sister and me. Papa Henri recounted how he had met him, fishing by the river Oise without knowing who he was until he went to see him at the Kommandantur.

"I am convinced that he protected Leon and Rachel. We will never know why, but it is not an accident that we escaped the roundups for more than two years," Papa Henri said.

Unfortunately, it was not the case for our cousin Charlot and twenty members of our family.

---

* Château de Compiègne was a French royal summer residence, completed in 1786.

Chapter 14

# Charlot

Sunday, July 19, 1942, on the same day and at the same time my parents were being arrested, a team of French gendarmes collaborating with the Gestapo was arresting Uncle Joseph and Aunt Madeleine Malmed.

They lived on rue du Puget, a fifteen-minute walk from our home. Their son Charles, nicknamed "Charlot" was three months away from his fourth birthday. My uncle and aunt had a good relationship with their next-door neighbors, the Baugis family. Mr and Mrs Baugis had three children, two daughters, Yvette and Rolande, and a son, Roger, ages twenty two, nineteen, and twenty six respectively. From time to time, Uncle Joseph asked Monsieur Baugis, who was quite handy, to help him with home repairs and my uncle did all the clothes alterations for the family. They were always happy to help each other.

Shortly after five o'clock that morning, surrounded by several French police officers, Uncle Joseph and Aunt Madeleine knocked at the door of their neighbors, the Baugis. Mr and Mrs Baugis were already awakened by the loud voices. Uncle Joseph threw himself at the feet of his neighbors and begged them to watch over Charlot. Mr and Mrs Baugis accepted without hesitation. Uncle Joseph gave them the key to their house. Without Mr and Mrs Baugis's compassion, Charlot would have been left alone in the house.

Never in their worst nightmare could any parents be imagined in such a position.

Uncle Joseph and Aunt Madeleine, full of emotion, kissed both Mr and Mrs Baugis before they were pulled away. They were not allowed to go into their home and kiss their son goodbye.

They would never see him again.

After their departure, Mrs Baugis ran into my aunt and uncle's house where little Charles was still sleeping.

The Baugis family and Charlot became quickly attached to each other. He was a beautiful and well-behaved little boy. Every day he accompanied Yvette, the oldest of the two daughters, to the Notre-Dame-de-Bon-Secours school, a private religious institution, where she was a kindergarten teacher. She developed a special bond with Charlot and he to her. She literally became his second mother.

Yvette's sister Rolande and her brother Roger worked in town. The Baugis family adored Charlot as their own son or grandson. Their commitment was the same as the commitment that Papa and Maman Ribouleau showed toward us. Monsieur Baugis also worked for the organization, the Aérostiers, with Papa and Maman Ribouleau.

More than two years went by. On January 19, 1944, a neighbor of the Baugis saw men in civilian clothes watching the street. He got on his bicycle and pedaled as fast as he could to Monsieur Baugis's workplace in order to alert him of the potential danger. He suspected these men were after little Charles. Everyone in the street loved Charlot and knew about his precarious situation.

By the time Mr Baugis rode his bicycle home the SS had come to the Baugis residence to arrest Charlot. He was not home. He was with Yvette at the school. A neighbor naively told the SS where they would find him.

The SS went to the school. They barged into Yvette Baugis' classroom and ordered Yvette and Charlot to follow them to the truck. Yvette, stupefied, protested the disruption and the scaring of the children in the classroom.

"Silence," ordered the SS officer. "You are hiding a Jew in your home. Do you know the punishment?"

Yvette kept on: "He is not even six years old; he is a baby. Take me instead. I can work, I can be useful," she told them.

"Shut up! You do not have Jewish blood. He does!" the SS officer answered.

"What about my class?" she asked.

The children in the classroom were so stunned and so scared that many wet their pants.

Yvette and Charlot were taken home to rue du Puget, where French collaborators and German soldiers were waiting.

Somehow, the entire Baugis family had returned home. When they saw Yvette and Charlot stepping down from the SS truck, they knew the danger they were facing.

*Charles ("Charlot"), Rachel, and Leon, 1941.*

Madame Baugis implored the SS officer to let her keep Charlot:

"He's not even six years old. Look at him. Does he look like a criminal?"

Monsieur Baugis, like Yvette and his wife had done earlier, begged:

"He is just a child. He has not committed any crime. Take me instead. I can be useful to the German army. Leave him with my wife."

Very well, said the officer in an arrogant tone:

"All of you get into the truck with the little Jew. You are all arrested for hiding a Jew."

In the end, the SS officer who did not have a written order to arrest anyone else besides the people on his list released the Baugis family and only Charlot was taken away.

Yvette hurriedly stuffed some clothes, food, a few cookies and candies in a bag.

"Here, my love, take this with you. Keep it close to you. You will be back soon. Be courageous." Madame Baugis told him, choking on the tears she could barely hold back, not wanting to frighten little Charles. She was kissing him and holding him tight against her breast as she had done so many times in the last two years. The Baugis family loved him so much. Each one of them was willing to give their life for him. An SS soldier tore her adored son from her and threw him in the truck like a bundle of dirty rags.

At that moment, Yvette had the premonition that she would never see him again.

Rolande Baugis, the youngest daughter, hurriedly grabbed her bike and followed the truck as best as she could. When the truck stopped, she was able to approach and ask the French civilian driver about their destination. He told Rolande that they were going to Chantilly, a town of twenty five thousand people about an hour away, as he had probably been told by the Germans. Rolande rushed to the train station to take the first train available to Chantilly. Somehow, she learned that the truck was not going to Chantilly but to Creil or Drancy. Both towns were also about an hour away from Compiègne. She left her bike behind and boarded the train. She ended up going to Drancy. Charlot was there, but she did not know. A wall separated them!

Rolande was not able to get into the detention center, which was by then under the control of the Gestapo. She could not even confirm that Charlot was there. Documents show that Charlot, not yet six years old, left Drancy by train via Creil on January 20, 1944, on convoy № 66. In this convoy, there were 221 children, 515 women, and 632 men, a total of 1368 people. A typical convoy transported about one thousand deportees. This one was exceptionally overcrowded.

It is difficult to imagine how this beautiful six-year-old child, three feet tall, and alone could have coped in this sealed cattle car for three or four days. What happened to him with not even enough room to sit, with forty children and probably more than sixty adults?

According to Suzanne Birnbaum,* who survived Auschwitz and who was in the same convoy as Charlot, the train left at 6:00 a.m. on Thursday morning and arrived in Auschwitz at about 12:30 a.m. Sunday morning, January 23rd. One hundred or more deportees had traveled three days in a train car with temperatures well below freezing, without food and practically no water.

She recalls that a little boy kept repeating:

"Maman, I am going to be afraid, Maman I am going to be afraid."

*Was it Charlot? Did he survive the transport? Was he trampled in this overcrowded cattle car? Did he die of fear? Did he die of distress? Did he die of thirst or did he die in the gas chamber or was he thrown alive in an open fire pit?*

We will never know.

Again, so many questions without answers ...

The doors of the cattle car, once locked in Creil, France from where they departed, reopened three days later in Auschwitz-Birkenau on a dark, icy night in January 1944. The detainees blinded by the spotlights heard the sound of barking dogs and saw hundreds of SS soldiers shouting orders and hitting people indiscriminately.

The people who were still alive were hurled onto the ramp along with their baggage or whatever was left of it. If Charlot was still alive then, which is doubtful, what was his reaction? How did he get from the train to the platform? What did he think; so small, confronted by the hellish sight of skeletons dressed in striped pajamas. The new, frightened and exhausted people were urged to jump on the platform as the soldiers hit them.

*Did he call for his parents that he had probably hoped to find at the end of this horrendous journey? Did he cry? Did he scream? Was he hit and killed by a SS soldier to shut him up? Was he pushed in a pit where they threw young children to die? Did he die in the horror of the gas chamber among dehumanized, naked adults and children trampling over each other searching for a gasp of air?*

I do hope with all my heart that he left this world during the transport without having witnessed the horrors of Auschwitz-Birkenau.

---

* Suzanne Birnbaum wrote her memoirs: *Une française juive est revenue* (Paris: Éditions du Livre français, 1946)

Whenever I am with my grandchildren, I often think of Charlot's tragic end. Charlot was one of the estimated 1.5 million who suffered the same fate.

I think of my own childhood and how close I came to this terrifying end. At such times, it is very hard for me to hold in my grief.

I have never talked to anyone until now about what atrocities might have happened to Charlot. I never did talk to my family about the fate of Jewish children under German occupation either. I did not want to frighten them or spoil their happiness. My grandchildren are a bit older now and hopefully, they will be able to handle the truth about the incredible atrocities that were committed against our family and millions of others.

It is important that they learn the history of the Holocaust.

It is important that they learn of the fate of the six millions Jews, and of the twenty members of our family who perished under the most barbaric conditions.

# Chapter 15

# Liberation

June 6, 1944.

The landing of the Allied forces in Normandy filled our hearts with hope. Victory seemed close.

Papa Henri rubbing his hands nervously smiled as he said: "The war will soon be over. We are winning."

The German troops were experiencing casualties. The schools converted into hospitals filled up quickly with wounded German soldiers. This was the first time we saw the vulnerability of the enemy. We were happy to see them suffer at last.

The increasingly frequent Allied air raids interrupted our classes more and more often.

Compiègne, a strategic railroad center was a target for the Allied forces. Though these bombings were extremely dangerous, ironically we were happy to know that the Allied forces were causing the Germans (the "boches," as we called them) heavy losses, despite the potential collateral damages to the civilians. When the sirens sounded for incoming Allied planes, we ran to the shelters. We had perfected the drill, well aware of the danger. Some of the children cried. Some kept their eyes closed tight, terrorized by the loud noise of the bombs exploding close by and the dust falling from the roof of the shelter. Via Radio London, we were aware of the advancing Allied forces. More and more rumors were circulating. How far away are the Allied troops? A day away? A week? A month? We felt the excitement of the liberation approaching. We also heard disconcerting rumors about preparations for a German counter offensive.

The question that came back very often was: "When is Hitler going to give up his diabolic enterprise?"

We were now confident that after four years of the horrible occupation and repression, freedom was near. For several days, waves of Allied planes drop bombs from ten thousand feet, day and night on the railroad station, about two miles from our home paralyzing rail and road transports of troops and ammunition. Some bombs missing their intended target caused deaths of civilians and destruction of homes. The Allied planes flew high to avoid being shot down by the German anti-aircraft guns. It made it very difficult to accomplish precision bombing.

At night, we heard the waves of Allied bombers flying to Germany. Blasting sirens warn the population of the incoming planes. We ran down the staircase several steps at a time, to the end of the garden where Papa Henri had built a bomb shelter. He dug a deep trench in front of the chicken coop, the roof was a sheet of corrugated metal covered with earth and tree branches for camouflage. The ceiling was so low that Papa Henri needed to bend over. A few steps cut in the earth led us inside. We sat down on small wooden benches. There was a small crate with a few bottles of water and some jars of preserved vegetables from the garden. We heard the whistling of the bombs falling for ten to fifteen seconds, which seemed forever. We had no idea where the bombs would end. We were frightened; yet at the same time felt secure. Fortunately, this shelter was never put to the true test.

Despite the fear of the bombing raids, we were happy that the Allied forces were so aggressive. Our hope of being reunited with our parents was becoming a reality. We were dreaming about the days when the German soldiers, the "doryphores," or beetles, as we also called them, would disappear from our country.

Since we were often awakened in the middle of the night, we slept with our clothes on. When we didn't have the time to run to the shelter, we took refuge in the cellar where we met with our neighbors from the first floor, the Clausse family.

The ladies sat while men remained standing. My sister and I were told to stand within the wooden structure that Papa Henri had built to reinforce the ceiling.

The air raids lasted about thirty minutes. All the lights were off. We heard rats scurrying around, which scared my sister more than the bombs we could hear exploding not far away. When the siren sounded the end of the alert, we breathed again and ran back to our beds, only to be awakening sometimes once or twice more that same night for another air raid scare.

Mid-1944, a new invention of mass destruction appeared. We started to see V-1 and then V-2 missiles flying high above. At first we had no idea what they were. They sounded like something between a whistle and a loud hum. It took a while to learn they were rockets, essentially flying bombs. They were designed to reach to England, mainly London, and kill as many people as possible. The first V-1 was launched at London on June 13, 1944. They had very short wings and spat fire. They inflicted much damage and caused many deaths. Sometimes, they exploded before they reached their destination. We feared them. When we heard their loud drone, we took cover in case one would explode above our neighborhood.

A major V-1 and V-2 launching facility, hidden in underground tunnels, was located about twenty miles away from us. Following an air raid that lasted several days, the Allied forces destroyed the launching facility. We heard the explosions and felt the earth shake, that far away from the site.

Beginning August 1944, bombardments intensified. On August 5th, four waves of twenty-four bombers each dropped bombs on our town's railroad station, which had been destroyed and rebuilt several times. The thundering sound was frightful. Craters of dirt and ashes had replaced buildings and single homes. The smoke was so thick that the whole town was in the dark for hours in daytime. We had no electricity for days. Thirty-seven civilians were killed and more than one hundred wounded. Entire families were buried in the rubbles. It was the sad ransom of war.

The next day, two hundred internees from the camp of Royallieu were brought to the area to repair the damaged railroad tracks under the oversight of the savage SS guards. While undergoing repairs, another wave of bombers dropped another hundred bombs on the site. The prisoners attempted to find shelter, but the SS soldiers stopped them by firing at them and killed ten of them. Another fifty died as a result of the bomb raid. In the panic of the shooting and the bombing, a few internees were able to escape, helped by courageous civilians.

Three days later, the Allied forces bombed the airfield of Margny-les-Compiègne a few miles away. This was the same airfield where Hitler landed in 1941, after ordering the burning of our town to avenge the capitulation of Germany in 1918.

Railroad transport from Compiègne was temporarily interrupted. Allied forces fighter planes were now aiming to destroy the railroad engines. Despite the enormous destruction, the Germans were able to assemble a deportation convoy. On August 17, 1944, two heroic resistance fighters prevented the train from departing by blowing up the rails a few miles north of the station.

The deportees were transferred to another train located beyond the damaged rails at a very small railroad station in the forest called Bellicart, a few miles away from Compiègne. Again, one hundred or more deportees were piled in each of the ten railroad cars.

It would be the last transport to reach an extermination camp.

During that torrid summer the deportees spent four days in the sinister train under the typical conditions, no water, no food, no toilets. The survivors in this infernal convoy trampled over the many who were dying or were dead. They waded in excrement. Very few made it to the destination, Buchenwald. And a very few of those who survived the trip were still alive when the American troops led by General George Patton liberated the camp on April 11, 1945.

On August 1, 1944, huge explosions were heard in Compiègne. The Germans were destroying their ammunition depots along with buildings, trucks, cars, and anything they could not take with them. Some civilians were killed for laughing at the retreating soldiers.

On the very day of the liberation of Paris, August 25, 1944, the SS in Drancy continued to organize a deportation convoy headed for an extermination camp. Fortunately, French railroad employees were able to sabotage the rail switching system and send the train to a different destination than intended. The Germans did not know that the train had been diverted to Péronne-Montdidier, a town that had been liberated a day or two earlier by the English troops. When the soldiers realized the train was not on the right tracks, it was too late. They attempted to escape, but most of them were captured. The English soldiers forced open the locks that sealed each railroad car and freed over one thousand deportees.

Compiègne was a stampede of the German troops fleeing. They stole bicycles and baby carriages to carry the spoils they had accumulated. A German soldier appropriated Papa Henri's bicycle. Very upset, he walked to the Kommandantur, the German Police station, to complain about the theft. He was told to take any bike that he could find in the building. Realizing what he had done and where he was, he picked the first bike he saw in the hallway and quickly pedaled home avoiding the main road. Afterwards he realized that he could have been shot just like other civilians who were seen smiling or laughing at the sight of soldiers fleeing or simply for accusing a German soldier of theft!

On the days preceding the Liberation, the bombing was replaced with heavy artillery fire from both armies. The American troops were advancing on the left bank of the river Oise while the Germans were retreating on the right bank. All day and night, shells were flying overhead. We were quite concerned of short-range misses. For three or four days, we remained in the cellar twenty-four hours a day. In the evening, we listened to Radio London. They confirmed the position of the Allied Forces, only a few miles from our town. We were overjoyed. Time seemed to stretch forever. We worried about being buried in the rubble of our building. The lack of anything to do, no game to play with, no book to read, was weighing on us all. When were we going to be liberated? *When will this war be over?*

We still feared a German counteroffensive.

The six of us were camping in the cellar, a fifteen-by-sixteen-foot room with one light bulb hanging from the ceiling, but not bright enough to read. A one by two-foot window flush with the sidewalk allowed little daylight. Six mattresses had been installed on the dirt. There was barely space to walk. With the continual noise of gunfire, it was very difficult to sleep. We used chamber pots as toilets. There was a water faucet in the laundry room next to the cellar. We did not dare leave the basement and go back up to the apartment. We were practically out of food.

On August 31, 1944, the town was silent. No more gun fire, no motor noise. An oppressive silence.

There was a strong burning smell. We learned later that the smell was coming from City Hall. Employees were burning compromising documents of their collaboration with the enemy.

It was a windy day with heavy rain showers and intermittent blue skies.

A memorable night began.

The artillery shelling came to a complete stop. Around two in the morning, we heard scattered gunfire and footsteps in our street. We thought that it could only be Allied soldiers. We did not recognize the sound of these footsteps. We were used to the awful clapping sound of the German boots. The footsteps we heard now were cushioned as though they were covered with rubber. All rubber products had been non-existent in France for the past three years.

It could only mean one thing.

At daybreak, one by one, the adults raised themselves to the narrow window located next to the ceiling of the cellar. Their view was so limited; they could only see the shoes of those who passed by.

We were asking ourselves: *Who is walking out there? It has to be Allied Forces soldiers. Who would dare go out at this time during the curfew?*

We didn't recognize the boots we saw.

René asked, "Are they American soldiers?"

Papa Henri responded, whispering. "I do not know for sure but it can only be them."

We did not dare call out, as they might have thought we had set a trap.

At about 6 a.m., unable to resist any longer the urge to find out whose boots we had seen from the cellar window, Papa Henri went up to the street and slowly opened the door to the street.

We heard a loud scream, "Montez vite, les Americains sont là!" Come up quickly. The Americans are here!

At 4:45 a.m. the outpost of the 28th division of the American Army had entered our town through the forest and came down the Boulevard Gambetta. It was renamed after the war "Boulevard des Etats-Unis," Boulevard of the USA.

We all ran up the basement stairs into the street. We were free!

Yes, the Americans were here. Yes, the "Boches" were gone.

Less than two hundred feet from our home, on the main road, rue de Paris, long columns of gigantic tanks, trucks pulling huge guns, jeeps that looked like toys, black and white soldiers were marching along pursuing the enemy fleeing northeast.

Homemade French and American flags appeared at every house window and in the hands of the people. Church bells were ringing loudly throughout the town. A huge clamor of joy came from the town center and spread quickly.

The children were running back and forth, giggling. We were exploding with the joy of knowing the ghastly enemy was being defeated.

*Was it possible? Were we dreaming?*

We wanted to touch the soldiers. We wanted to embrace them. We wanted to thank them for delivering us from the inhumane Nazis. It had been four years since the war started, four years of misery, four years of starvation, four years of fear every minute of every day, four years of despair hoping for this day.

Compiègne was liberated on September 1, 1944. In another month, I would be seven years old.

I ran home, picked tomatoes and carrots from our garden and ran back and gave the fresh vegetables to the soldiers. They ate them on the spot. From the tank turrets and the trucks, they threw us chocolates and chewing gum, things I had never seen nor tasted.

It was difficult to comprehend and believe that at last we were free. I was too young when the war started to know how it felt to be free.

People who did not know each other fell into each other's arms and kissed and cried together.

"Leon! Our parents will be here soon!" My sister Rachel was screaming, tears streaming on her beautiful face as she squeezed me hard against her.

We held on to each other and sobbed for a long time, incapable of holding our emotions any longer. We had endured so much.

Finally, we allowed ourselves to feel a happiness we did not know existed.

"The nightmare is over, my dear children," said Maman Suzanne in a reassuring voice. "We will live again. Your parents will be back soon."

The joy, the emotions were so strong, I could not stop trembling. I shook from nervous laughter, blinded by tears.

For the first time since our parents were taken away from us, July 19, 1942, I was not scared!

Chapter 16

# "They are not coming back"

For hours, we watched as hundreds, maybe thousands of tanks, jeeps, and trucks filled with American soldiers passed by our street. The crowd was singing, laughing, offering fruits and fresh vegetables to the soldiers.

Compiègne was liberated at last!

The enemy was defeated, but Hitler would not give up. The Allied forces continued the offensive. Hitler persisted in pursuing his diabolical dream. Still, a semblance of normality emerged in the liberated areas. Some civilian cars, mostly commercial, were now circulating. People were walking and stopping to talk to each other. The cafés were reopening. We were going to school on a regular basis. Fear was gone. We were waiting for our parents' return any day now.

Anticipating their return was consuming our thoughts.

My early memories start with the arrest of our parents. Since then, I had lived in semi-hiding, fearful of the Germans, denunciation and plagued by nightmares.

What was a normal life? I had never known one. Everyone was happy. People were laughing at last and talking about the future.

So a normal life must be when people are happy, smiling, and laughing.

We no longer jumped at any unusual noise from the street or from creaks in the staircase. We no longer feared our neighbors, our friends, our teachers, our townsfolk.

We were waiting impatiently to hear from our parents. They must be already liberated by now or would be soon. They were going to ring the doorbell anytime. Probably not. They would come up the stairs and knock at the door. It was possible that they had sent a card or a letter. The mail was not working reliably yet. No, they would appear before their letter or card arrived. We had not heard from them since the card received from Drancy, written July 23rd, 1942, when our mother asked for warm clothes, cooking utensils, and food. That was more than two years ago. We were certain that they suffered from lack of food like we did, probably worse than we did since they did not have a garden like we did. They probably had lost much weight. *Would we recognize them? Any day now.*

Nazi Germany was not yet vanquished but we were certain Hitler would ask for an armistice soon. Radio London reported the systematic destruction of all major industrial cities in Germany. We were guardedly optimistic. We still kept hearing rumors of a major counter-offensive. We knew that if the Germans were to return to our town very few of us would survive.

Trains were no longer operating. Road transportation was at a standstill while the Allied forces did the repairs and removed the barriers and mines the Germans had left behind.

No deportees from Compiègne had returned yet. A few more weeks and they would all come back said Papa Henri with an encouraging smile.

His reassuring words filled us with joy and hope.

The day after the Liberation of Compiègne, for the first time since our parents departed, Rachel and I went up to our former apartment. René and Marcel still slept there every night. Everything was in the same order as it was when our parents left: the furniture, clothes in the drawer and in the small closet, and cooking utensils in the kitchen. Everything was clean and ready for our parents' return.

We stayed a long time in our apartment, looking at the family photos. It was very emotional. Soon, we would be looking at the same photos together with Papa and Maman. I was less than five years old when I last saw them. I remembered my father to be tall and strong and my mother so beautiful with her long braided hair. Their faces had slowly faded from my memory. However, looking at the pictures I could remember them. I could hear their voices, their laughs and the songs that my mother used to sing when she was free and happy. I again had problems falling asleep. I was so impatient to see them again. Though, I was disappointed; they had not come back yet. *Where are they? They would come home tomorrow or the day after for sure.*

*What would I do when I saw them? Should I run to them and jump in their arms? No, I should not do that. They would be exhausted from their long trip and two years of hard work and depravation. Yes, I know. I would approach them slowly. I would encircle both their legs with my small arms and snuggle against them. We would stay like that, my eyes raised to watch their faces. Yes, we would stay like that for a long time. Later, I would climb onto my father's lap and settle down, my head against his chest and I would be at peace, at last. He would caress my hair and tell me how much he missed me.*

I did not know then that I would be waiting the rest of my life for that moment.

Our Uncle Charles Blum, my mother's older brother, came back from Germany where he had been held prisoner for five years. Thanks to his false name, "Blumi" instead of Blum, he escaped the extermination camps. Working for a German carpenter provided him with a roof and some protection from dangerous and hard labor. Every morning, he and other prisoners walked from the barracks to their assigned jobs, returning after a twelve-hour day.

Somehow, the prisoners knew about the impending liberation of the camp. A few days before he was liberated, Uncle Charles became very concerned that the German soldiers might react violently. He feared they might take hostages and shoot them in anger for the defeat of Germany. He hid in the barn of his employer.

Uncle Charles had very little knowledge of what had gone on in the world during his five-year captivity. He knew nothing about the atrocities committed by the Nazis. He knew nothing about the exterminations and the savage killing of civilian hostages, of underground fighters, of Communists, of gypsies and others during the occupation of most of Europe by Nazi Germany.

Upon his return to his home in Saint-Quentin, he expected to find his wife Sarah and his two daughters, but there was no one home and it looked like no one had been there for a long time. He ended up connecting with his niece, Hélène Gerbaez. She told Uncle Charles that his wife, Sarah, fled to the south of France in 1940 a few days before the invasion and was probably there. Hélène also mentioned that she had not heard from the rest of our family since 1942. She thought most of the family had been deported but did not know where. He was awestruck when she told him about the Holocaust rumors she had heard. It took months for the world to learn and to believe the scale of the crimes committed by Nazi Germany. The magnitude of the atrocities was beyond human comprehension.

Before the war, the Blum and the Malmed families were living north of Paris. When the Germans invaded France from the North via the Belgian border, civilians fled south toward Paris, which they believed would never be occupied. The rapidly advancing enemy forces made them change their mind, and most of them continued on south as fast as they could, for as long as they could find fuel and were able to drive through the overcrowded roads littered with broken-down cars, horse carriages, and other obstacles.

In the spring of 1940, my Aunt Sarah Blum drove her van stocked with the merchandise they used to sell on the open markets. She had never been south of Paris prior to this trip. Though it was difficult, nearly impossible, she was able to find food and gas in exchange for merchandise along the way. After two or three days of strenuous driving she ran out of gas. Aunt Sarah, with her mother Boubé and the younger of her two daughters Madeleine, was about two hundred and fifty miles south of Paris in a village called Lalinde. She was able to find an empty barn where she hid the van. Like her, thousand of refugees were searching for food and gas. She was concerned about theft. A kind person at the village town hall was able to locate a one-large-room apartment. They lived there for the duration of the war.

Due to the immediacy of the invasion and evacuation orders, Aunt Sarah had not been able to locate her eldest daughter who was in school at the time. Schools had been provided with buses and were ordered to evacuate immediately. There was no time to advise the parents. In those days telephones were located at the Post Office. With the help of the Red Cross, Rachel, Aunt Sarah's daughter was located and reunited with her mother in Lalinde. For the next four years, the four of them were able to survive by slowly selling the merchandise they had been able to take with them when they left Saint-Quentin.

In July 1942, Uncle Zelman Malmed and his son Jacques came to live with them in Lalinde. At the beginning of the occupation, Uncle Zelman was the one who thought that Paris with its several million residents would be a good place to hide. Shortly after the invasion it became very difficult and close to impossible to travel without a special permit. Jewish people were forbidden to even move within their own town. During the Vel' d'Hiv' roundup,* the French police came to arrest the entire Zelman Malmed family. It was a warm day and windows were opened. They heard noise in front of the building. The French police were opening up doors and barking orders. They were prepared for an arrest, as people disappeared on a daily basis. Aunt Sarah Malmed thought they were arresting men only. She and her daughters would be safe. She told Uncle Zelman and her son Jacques to go and hide in an unoccupied maid's room several floors up, a place only known by a few.

But this time the French police had orders to arrest men, women, and children, and they obeyed zealously. Aunt Sarah Malmed and her two daughters, Ida and Sonia, were taken away to the Vel' d'Hiv'. With so many people to pick up, the police did not take the time to search the building in that instance. Aunt Sarah Malmed and 14-year-old Ida left Drancy for Auschwitz by Convoy № 13. Sonya, 22, left with Convoy № 16. Since the documents show that they were not tattooed on arrival, they either died in the train or were gassed on arrival at the Auschwitz-Birkenau extermination camp.

Uncle Zelman and Jacques were able to leave Paris and slip into the so-called "Free Zone" or "Zone Libre," a partition of the French territory established at the Armistice signed in Compiègne on June 22, 1940. The Free Zone extended about one hundred miles south of Paris to the Mediterranean Sea and was administered by the French government of Marshal Pétain, based in Vichy.

Several weeks later Uncle Zelman and Jacques made their way to Lalinde, in the department of Dordogne, where they joined Aunt Sarah Blum.

They were now six people living in a single room with the proceeds of the clothes left in the van and money that Zelman had brought with him.

Shortly after their arrival, Uncle Zelman and my cousin Jacques were denounced. The French police in that area had orders to arrest only Jewish men, which was fortunate for Aunt Sarah, her mother and two daughters. Both Uncle Zelman and Jacques ended up at the detention camp of Riversaltes in the cold winter of 1942–1943. They were housed in an unheated, empty warehouse used at one time for the maintenance of steam locomotives. They were then transferred to Arles-sur-Tech. Jacques was given a job as a janitor for the French camp police. One evening as he was cleaning the empty offices, he noticed a book of leave permits lying on a desk. He found the rubber stamps in the drawer to allow internees to leave the camp in rare cases of extreme emergency. Without hesitation he filled out two permits, one for his father and one for himself.

Uncle Zelman refused to leave the camp for fear of being shot for stealing the permits. Jacques left immediately and managed to travel to a friend of the family in the town of Agen a hundred miles away. He stayed there a few days before deciding what to do next. The police were looking for him. Had he been captured, he probably would have been shot. He made his way to Spain, supposedly a neutral country under Franco's dictatorship at the time, with the intention to go to North Africa and join the Allied Forces. He survived the crossing of the Pyrénées* on foot with the help of a smuggler. Jacques paid the smuggler's expensive fee with the money he and his father had sown in their clothes before leaving Paris. During the difficult crossing of the Pyrénées a mother and her teenage daughter were so exhausted that they were not able to keep up with the group and were left behind. Who knows what happened to them? As Jacques was coming off the mountains, he was arrested by the Spanish border police and put in jail. Two months later, he was liberated by an American intermediary who traded a few bags of wheat for the release of a couple of prisoners, including Jacques. A French organization in Spain helped him join the French army in Morocco where he enlisted to fight the Germans. He never had the opportunity to do so, as the war in North Africa ended shortly after his arrival, in May 1943. Jacques survived the Holocaust. He passed away in 2011 at the age of 88.

---

* The Pyrénées are mountains of 3,500 feet average height that extend from the Mediterranean Sea to the Atlantic Ocean, forming a natural frontier between France and Spain.

Before the police discovered that Jacques was missing from the internment camp, Uncle Zelman decided to leave the camp using the forged permit Jacques had prepared for him. Not knowing where to go, he returned to the home of his sister, Aunt Sarah Blum, in Lalinde at the risk of being arrested again. Fortunately, he remained there in hiding until the town was liberated.

My other cousins, most of them from Saint-Quentin, also suffered similar difficulties during World War II, hiding wherever they could with the help of courageous and unselfish people.

Salomon spent the years of occupation in the south of France in a number of orphanages. His mother Gela Kibel and his stepfather Joseph Borowicz were deported in February of 1944 to Auschwitz-Birkenau and gassed on arrival.

Jean, Georges, Hélène, and Maurice, accompanied by their parents, Ida and Abraham Gerbaez hid in farms in the southwest of France. Uncle Abraham was arrested on the construction site where he worked by the French police, who again served their German masters. He was deported to Majdanec by Convoy № 51 and exterminated.

Soon after the Armistice was signed, Aunt Sarah Blum learned, with the help of the Red Cross, that her husband, Uncle Charles, had come back unhurt from the prison camp where he had been held for the last five years. She immediately went back to Saint-Quentin. At that time, they still had no idea of what happened to the rest of the family. They then learned that the Gerbaez family had been hiding in the south of France. Uncle Charles was able to find them, and bring Tante Ida and cousins Jean, George, and Maurice back to Saint-Quentin.

The next task was to find the rest of the family. They inquired at the Town Hall of Compiègne. They were told that a family named Ribouleau had hidden Rachel and Léon Malmed since 1942 but they had no information regarding Srul and Chana nor about Joseph and Madeleine and their son Charles Malmed.

At last the Second World War Armistice was signed on May 8, 1945. In Compiègne like in all other towns in France, people celebrated the victory. Church bells rang for several days. People danced in the streets. A joyful ceremony took place at the forest clearing where the First World War Armistice—with Germany capitulating—was signed, and the Second World War Armistice, when Hitler came to witness the capitulation of France in June 1940. A huge man-made fire burned in the clearing, aimed at erasing the terror of the last five years.

Everyone joined the festivities in town. Happiness was on everyone's face. The dark years were behind them. The "doryphores"* had fled. Life had sprung back like tree buds in the spring, and it was springtime. The trees were in bloom. The enemy was gone. Fear was gone. We could walk freely without the fear of being arrested or shot.

*Where were our parents? No one knew. The authorities did not know. What should we do? What was going to happen to us?*

In December of 1944 we learned that our parents, as well as my Uncle Joseph, Aunt Madeleine, and cousin Charlot, had been sent to a deportation camp, without any other information as to which camp and their current status.

It took several more months after the end of the war before the horrors of Germany's abominable crimes were known. I was almost eight years old. The radio broadcasts started to describe what the Allied forces found when they liberated the camps. Photos in the newspapers started to appear. They were hidden from me. I was watching the street. I was still listening to any unusual noise. *Papa and Maman would come back any moment. They would. All the camps are now liberated. Where are they?*

The world was discovering the magnitude of the crimes committed against humanity, of the human suffering of millions in the many extermination camps, Auschwitz-Birkenau, Majdanec, Mauthausen, Buchenwald, Dachau, Ravensbrück, Sobibor, Treblinka, Chelmo, Maly Trostenets, Belzec, and others in Germany and eastern Europe. The newspapers published the pictures of heaps of bodies, naked, thrown in pits, or laying piled up everywhere in the camps. They found mounts of ashes. They found emaciated, gaunt

---

* The German soldiers were hated. The French people called them different nasty names such as: *doryphores, schleus, boches*. The *doryphore* is a devastating beetle that eats potato plants. *Schleus* and *boches* did not have any signification except that it felt good to say it under your breath whenever we saw a German soldier. At home, we never talked about the Germans like German was not a nationality; we referred to them as the "boches" or the "schleus" as if they were viruses.

human beings who could hardly walk, their legs and arms looking like sticks. The soldiers could not believe what they saw—walking skeletons, living dead.

It took several weeks, months, for the first few French survivors to arrive in Paris. They were directed to the Hotel Lutetia. It was the main site in Paris to reunite with relatives. This hotel had been the SS headquarters with the most feared criminal Nazi militia.

The deportees came back from another world, another planet. Families searching for their loved ones camped in front of the hotel day and night, awaiting the return of spouses, sons, daughters, parents, and relatives. Families also waited at the Paris northern and eastern train stations. They questioned the returnees but only got exhausted grunts and shrugs. These poor souls were not able to talk about the hell and the horrors they had endured for months and a few for years. People screamed the names of their missing ones. Billboards were set up where photos and messages were posted. The exhausted deportees pushed them away in desperation. Their minds were still in the camps. *How could they tell these people that over there, from where they came out alive by some miracle, there were no names, no human faces.* They survived one minute at a time. They died. They disappeared. They hoped to stay alive another day. They were numbers, dehumanized, shaved heads, dressed in striped pajamas in winters and summers; they had shoes too small or too big. They were slaves of what Germany called the Grand Reich.

Papa Henri and Maman Ribouleau contacted the Red Cross many times to locate our parents. Alas, they were unsuccessful. Papa and Maman had vanished from the face of the earth.

We received many compassionate looks. Several times a day, I heard "poor children" whispered around us. Rachel and I fell into a denial mode and we no longer spoke about our parents. It was too painful and too emotional. We were concerned about our immediate future but we did not dare ask questions. What would happen to us if our parents did not come back? We were convinced they would come back. Although the Ribouleau family protected us and gave us their affection, we always felt that the situation was temporary. Our parents would come back and Papa Henri and Maman Suzanne would become our cherished Aunt and Uncle. It took a very long time to accept the fact that our parents might not return. I was now allowed to look at the pictures of the returning deportees in the newspapers. I could not bring myself to see my parents in such state. No, those living dead with gaunt face, deep sunken eyes, arms and legs without flesh with festering sores, and shaved heads had nothing to do with my parents. No, my parents could never look like them. Impossible! Our parents must be in Russia, maybe in a hospital or a shelter to regain strength before they come back to us. They are still looking like the photos they left with us.

Wild rumors circulated on the fate of the deportees. Maybe after so many years of incarceration our parents were confused and went back to Poland where they were born. Maybe they could not find transportation. Maybe they had been tortured and as a result they had memory loss? I kept hoping for a long time. It took me many years to accept they had died under such atrocious conditions.

Today, what I have left from my parents is my father's ring, which I wear all the time, and an old-fashioned pocket watch in a leather case that belonged to my father as well. Every so often, I look at the watch, thinking of my father rewinding it. My sister also has a few items from our parents. The photos they left are the most precious items. The photos have aged, but our parents have not. They are still as handsome and pretty as the day they were taken away from us. Their children, their hair, their teeth, their souls, and their lives were stolen. Stolen were their future and the joys of seeing their children growing and becoming a woman and a man. Instead their bodies were burned and used to fertilize the fields of the Grand Reich.

How can I ever accept such an end to my parents' life? How can I ever forgive the perpetrators of such crimes?

Two years after the end of the war, the French government issued a Certificate of disappearance for both our parents dated July 9, 1947. They were declared absent. If they did not reappear within five years, a Death Certificate would be sent to us. We eventually learned that they were deported from the Drancy Internment camp near Paris to Auschwitz, Poland, ironically their native country, on July 29, 1942, ten days after their arrest in Compiègne.

On July 9, 2009 I received a letter, sixty-seven years after their deportation, from an international research organization I had contacted many years ago. It said that my father was tattooed upon his arrival at the Auschwitz-Birkenau concentration camp with the number 54315. It also said that he was still alive on July 1, 1944. The Soviet army liberated Auschwitz on January 24, 1945, nearly seven months later! As for my mother, since she was not tattooed, she either died during the transport from Drancy to Auschwitz or was gassed and cremated immediately upon arrival.

Both died in Poland, a country they left more than a decade earlier for a better future which they found in France. France had welcomed them and allowed them to start their own business, to raise a family and be happy. France was free of pogroms,* anti-Semitism, and government restrictions. They had lived ten years of happiness together with their two children they adored.

In 1942, they were brutally taken away, deported to a death camp where my mother was murdered immediately and my father enslaved and eventually died. They suffered an ignoble death engineered by Nazi Germany, whose viciousness and motives cannot be comprehended to this day.

---

*A pogrom is an organized massacre of helpless people; from a Russian word meaning "to wreak havoc, to demolish violently." Historically, the term refers to violent attacks by local non-Jewish populations on Jews, sometimes with government and police encouragement. Jewish victims were raped, murdered and their property looted.

# Chapter 17

# Being Jewish

I hated being Jewish. I did not understand what it meant to be Jewish. I could not see any difference between a Jewish person and another person. It did not make sense to me.

Who was this person, Jesus Christ? Where did I hear that the Jews were responsible for his death? What was the relationship between him and the Jewish people? I even heard that he was a Jew. The Jewish people must have committed abominable crimes to arouse such hatred and such a need for vengeance that seems to have endured for the last 2000 years, to this day.

All I knew was that being Jewish was at the origin of my parents murder. I was forever traumatized.

I was lucky to find a warm nest where I was loved. After my parents' arrest, it took a number of months before I could get used to this new and different environment. At the time I did not know that my parents were taken away for the sole reason that they were Jewish. It is only when I turned six or seven, when the SS came in 1944 to arrest my sister and me, that I realized that the words "Jews," "Israélites," or "Jude" meant bad news. Starting in July 1942, for almost three years, we were in a state of constant fear. We were hunted. It became acute the last year of the war. We miraculously escaped several arrest attempts by the Germans. Maman Suzanne had prepared two bags with warm clothes and some food. They were ready, in the entryway of our apartment in case the SS came to pick us up. I was old enough to understand the curse, the danger and possibly death associated with the words "Jews" or "Israélites."

I kept asking myself what the Jews could have done to provoke such reprisals. I was too shy to ask aloud. Maybe I was afraid of the answer. Seventy years later I am no longer too shy to ask the question. I do ask the question, but I still do not have an answer.

When I realized that my parents might not be coming back I was angry and did not want anything to do with the word "Jew." I did not want to become Catholic either. Just like Papa Henri and Maman Suzanne, few people in France practice religion. But I certainly did not want to be Jewish. I could not stand any longer the pitiful expressions of the people when they talked to me. They all meant well and were simply trying to show their compassion. I wanted to be "normal." I wanted to be "like everyone else." Not so simple though.

What that meant to me at the time was to melt into the masses. I did not like the feeling of being "different." I did not like the sad expressions of the adults as they repeated "poor child, look what they did to the Jews." Those words would make me feel extremely uncomfortable. I avoided the people who were too kind to me and tried their best to comfort me in my distress.

When the war ended I began to live a life that was close to "normal." My sister and I waited for our parents' return, still. We kept thinking: "What will happen to us if they do not come back?"

Very few Jewish families from Compiègne survived the Holocaust. The ones who escaped deportation and returned to Compiègne resumed their pre-war occupations. They were able to move back into their homes and businesses, unlike the Jews who returned to their homes and places of business in the Eastern countries, where many were beaten or even killed by the people who had stolen their properties.

What seems unbelievable is that very few Jewish people who survived the war talked about the events of the war. Like my sister and me, they probably did not want to bring the emotions to the surface. Some survivors even carried a feeling of guilt for having survived.

Why were they alive when so many of their family, friends and neighbors were gone?

Why did they survive?

Whenever someone brought up my Jewish roots, not even in a negative way, I would freeze. I became paralyzed. I could not think, speak or move. Blood rushed to my cheeks. I was ashamed. Why? Yes, why?

For many years, I could not free myself of this "malaise."

I needed to prove that this "poor child" would be able to build a normal life like everyone else.

I was determined to obtain a skill that I would enjoy instead of rushing into a situation from which I might not be able to escape. I was caught between the desire to stop being a financial burden to the Ribouleau family and the desire to pursue a higher education.

During my teenage years and during the twenty-eight months I spent in the French Air Force, I was not subjected to anti-Semitism. However, I was always on guard.

Shortly after being demobilized in 1963 from the French Air Force, I accepted a job offer from a large tire manufacturer in Clermont-Ferrand, a town located in a beautiful region of Auvergne. The company policy was to train and evaluate new engineering recruits for a year while working on solutions to manufacturing problems and enhancements before being assigned to a specific department.

One of my co-workers, a man in his thirties found out or guessed that I was Jewish. Several times a day, when no one else was around in the office, he would say in a low voice but loud enough so I could hear him clearly: "You are a *youpin*\*—there is one among us. You are one of them. Get out of here." When there were other people in the office, he would look at me insistently with an ugly grin on his face with the sole purpose of making me feel uncomfortable and wanting to leave. I must admit that he was successful. Again I was paralyzed, incapable of reacting. Since I had never talked to anyone about such situations, I did not know how to deal with it. I had no example to follow. I never brought it up to my supervisor. That is what this ugly individual counted on. At the time I did not think the management of the company would understand. And I did not want anyone to know I was Jewish. I was still under the spell of being ashamed of my origins. In hindsight I was so wrong, so very wrong. I did myself harm and probably did a disservice to my employer by not revealing the demeanor of this racist employee.

The behavior of that miserable person helped me make the difficult decision to leave France. I hoped that in America, being Jewish would be accepted. I hoped that people would judge me for my

---

\* Demeaning word for a Jew.

character and behavior, not for my family heritage, which I did not choose. My hopes and dreams were answered. I have been living in the United States and not once have I felt that I was treated any differently than any other person because of my background. Racism unfortunately exists in most countries.

It took many years before I became comfortable with the words "Juif" or "Jew." I am no longer paralyzed by such simple words as I had been the first twenty-six years of my life. When I lived in France, if someone intended to hurt me by calling me "sale Juif" (dirty Jew) I did not know what to say. How can two words be so hurtful? Why did I care so much in the first place?

Literally I know that I was not "dirty." Yes I am "Jewish," so what? Yet I became defensive. I know that those simple words were said to hurt my feelings. I always wondered for what reason anyone would utter these words without provocation with the sole purpose of upsetting another human being.

Same with the words "You are one of them." The tone, the mimicry, and the looks hurt terribly when someone like me lacked the maturity and the confidence to respond with dignity.

All of it is now behind me. I am finally free of the heavy burden of fearing racism and ever present potential humiliation.

As to the religious side, for many years our family has celebrated Christmas, Chanukah, Easter, Passover, New Year's, and the Jewish New Year. I am not a religious observer ; however, I do enjoy the traditions, customs, and opportunities to bring our family together.

Today my shame of being Jewish is totally gone. I am proud of my heritage. A heritage that tragically has claimed the life of my parents and more than twenty members of my family. A heritage that has caused the murder of six million human beings who were reduced to ashes and smoke for only one reason, because they were born Jewish.

I no longer struggle with saying "I am Jewish," such simple words that I could not pronounce for so many years!

# Chapter 18

# Saint-Quentin

At last, the war was over. We were told the unimaginable: "our parents may not come back." This was impossible to accept or even comprehend.

My sister and I were very concerned about what would happen next.

"Would we be able to stay with the family that protected us for the last three years?" Papa Henri and Maman Suzanne were our family, the only family we knew. We had bonded.

The answer set in motion yet another set of traumatic events that would shake up our future.

Uncle Charles and Aunt Sarah Blum had decided that my sister and I must go and live with them. After discovering the fate of so many members of our family, they probably felt it was their duty to regroup the family. The crisis that ensued revealed that forcing us to live with them was not exactly what they had thought would be a smooth phase-in. They had located my cousin Salomon (Sali) and brought him to their home. Sali was ten years old when the war ended. He had escaped extermination and was living at the time in an orphanage close to Paris, one of many he had stayed in during the war.

In mid-1945, Uncle Charles and Aunt Sarah came, unannounced, to our home in Compiègne and demanded, aggressively, that we, Rachel and I, leave with them immediately. This encounter began a string of actions that would drastically change the lives of my sister and me. I was terrified. I was reliving the day of our parents' arrest. Again, someone wanted to tear us away from parents we loved.

Showing up without prior notice shocked Papa Henri and Maman Suzanne. They did not know these people and were not even aware of them. Without any preamble these strangers insisted on taking us immediately—the children Papa and Maman Ribouleau had protected and cared for and whose lives they had saved. They had made a promise to our parents and intended to keep it. We were still waiting for our parents' return. They might be alive and when they came back, we would be here. The Ribouleaus categorically refused to let Uncle and Aunt Blum take us. I was trembling and hanging onto Maman Suzanne's dress. Aunt Sarah frightened me.

Neither Rachel nor I wanted to leave this family. We were happy with the Ribouleau family. I must have been about three years old when I last saw Uncle Charles and Aunt Sarah, and I did not remember them at all. I felt no affection and certainly no desire to go and live with these strangers.

Aunt Sarah had survived the war on her own, and taken care of her aging mother and two daughters. She was a resourceful and tenacious person. She could not understand why the Ribouleaus refused to let us go with them. She was very upset. As they were leaving she screamed:

"We will take you to court. You have no right to these children. They belong to us. They are our blood; their father is my brother; their mother is my husband's sister."

Papa and Maman Ribouleau were shocked. After all the sacrifices the Ribouleau family had made for us, Uncle Charles and Aunt Sarah threatened to take them to court! Papa Henri and Maman Suzanne faced a tough fight which would mean more anguish and untold expense. They lived paycheck to paycheck. Due to the high price of food and all other commodities, the cost of living remained very high for several years after the war ended, and they were still paying the rent for our parents' apartment.

A week later, as Rachel and I were leaving school to walk home for lunch, Uncle Charles was standing close to the school gate. There were many children coming out but very few adults. We saw him but ignored him. We started to walk as fast as we could without running. He caught up with us, grabbed me by the arm and pulled me toward his van saying loudly:

"Both of you, you come with me, quick."

Rachel was hysterical and tried to free me from his grip. I kicked him in the leg, and I was able to shake free before we reached the van. Rachel and I ran home as fast as we could, Rachel shouting, "Quick Leon, quick."

I was as terrified by this kidnapping attempt as I was when the Germans came to arrest us. We arrived home out of breath. We told Papa Henri and Maman Suzanne what had happened. They were appalled.

"Will they be coming to take us tomorrow?" I asked between sobs.

"No, they will not come back," said Papa Henri, sounding doubtful.

Papa Henri and Maman Suzanne decided not to go to the police. I never asked why. I would not have been surprised if I had been told that they did not trust the police. Instead, they met with the mayor of Compiègne, "Baron James de Rothschild." He was a kind and fair person. He offered to have Rachel and I stay at his home until the situation quieted down. He resided in a large pavilion, more of a small castle in Vieux-Moulin, a beautiful village nestled in the middle of the forest, about ten miles from Compiègne's town center.

Our stay was like a vacation. While we were there we did not go to school. The servants pampered us. We spent more than a month living a life of luxury. The "Baron" and the "Baronness" were the only occupants outside of the help.

When we went back home to 17 rue Saint-Fiacre we learned that a court date had been set for a Family Council requested by the Blum family. Their goal was to take us away from the Ribouleau family. The Ribouleaus asked us with whom we wanted to be. Our answer was with them. They sensed that we would not be happy with our uncle and aunt. They did not want us to leave either. I imagine they remembered the looks on our parents' faces and the promise they had made to them.

Fear of losing our second parents was there again.

The Family Council took place at the Court House. The judge was seated on a high platform. The set-up was very imposing and frightening. I sat a few feet away from the foot of the platform and had to hold my head way back in order to see the judge. Rachel and I were not asked which family we wanted to live with. Minors did not have rights to voice their opinion, and we were too intimidated to say anything. Papa Henri and Maman Suzanne sat behind us. I would turn around often to observe their reaction to different exchanges that I did not understand. Papa Henri would give me a wink and Maman Suzanne a smile indicating that all was going well. Besides, we were certain of the outcome. Aunt Ida who was not on good terms with Uncle Charles and her sister, Sarah Blum, at the time, had assured us that she would vote in favor of us staying with the Ribouleau family.

She was very poor, having to raise three boys on her own. Papa Henri and Maman Suzanne had paid her train fare from Saint-Quentin to Compiègne as well as her hotel room and her restaurant meals.

All we needed was one vote, which she had pledged to us.

The judge asked Aunt Ida if she favored that we be entrusted to the Ribouleau or the Blum family. Aunt Sarah, who was seated next to Aunt Ida, turned to her and said something in Yiddish. The only other person there who understood Yiddish was Uncle Charles. What Aunt Sarah said to Aunt Ida must have been very threatening. We never knew what was said, but it was powerful enough for Aunt Ida to turn very pale.

"Silence!" screamed the judge at Aunt Blum "or I will ask you to leave."

It was too late.

Aunt Ida, white as a ghost, said almost inaudibly, "They should go with the Blum family."

"No, no, she made an error!" I said.

I felt terribly weak. It was a nightmare. I cannot go with these people. No! No!

I could never leave Papa and Maman Ribouleau. I could not live with these people who were so mean, people I did not even know. I was terrorized.

The judge said: "From now on, Rachel and Leon Malmed are in the custody of their uncle and aunt, Charles and Sarah Blum. The case is closed." He looked at Papa and Maman Ribouleau sympathetically and walked out.

They were frozen in their seat. They could not believe what had just happened.

The verdict pronounced by the judge would change our destiny.

We returned to 17 rue Saint Fiacre, followed by Uncle and Aunt Blum. Almost like the French gendarmes who came to arrest our parents four years before, they waited impatiently on the sidewalk while we packed a suitcase. We were not prepared at all for such an outcome.

Again, we were forced against our will to leave the people we loved, the people who by now I called Papa and Maman, the people who had protected us against brutal enemies, the people who had saved our lives, the people who had risked their lives, the people who had sacrificed so much for us.

Aunt Sarah who had come up to the landing, was urging us to leave with no concern for our distress. As we were hurried to their van that would take us away from our beloved family. Papa Henri tried to sound cheerful when he said: "We will see you soon" while Maman Suzanne, cried "my children!"

She could not say any more. She was holding on to both of us tightly but had to let go.

Uncle Charles, indifferent to our grief, grabbed us forcefully and pulled us. We were overwhelmed with despair.

The Blum family lived in Saint-Quentin, a town of about 40,000 people, fifty miles north of Compiègne. Not being a major railroad center, the town was spared from the German and Allied bombing. Most houses and buildings were made of red bricks dating from World War I.

Their home was a small two-story with a living room, a small kitchen downstairs and four tiny bedrooms upstairs including a closet/bedroom. The house had only one water faucet, in the kitchen over the sink. There was no bathroom. Bathrooms were luxuries only found in wealthy homes. Every morning, eight people washed their faces with the same washcloth. There was a glass-covered patio—fifteen by fifteen feet. The outdoor toilet was in one corner of the small courtyard, where a few hens were running around with their droppings everywhere.

The street was dirty. The street gutters acted as sewers. The dirt was washed out only when it rained. Comfort was nonexistent. Eight of us lived in that small house: Uncle Charles, Aunt Sarah, my paternal grandmother "Boubé", my cousins, the daughters of Uncle Charles and Aunt Sarah, Rachel and Madeleine, my cousin Salomon, and my sister Rachel. I shared a small, narrow bed with my cousin Salomon. Our bedroom was a converted windowless junk closet.

Rachel, my cousin, the oldest of Uncle Blum and Aunt's daughters, had contracted meningitis when she was an infant. It left her mentally handicapped. She never went to school. Her younger sister, Madeleine was my age—a pretty girl who was always nice to us.

The adults and teenagers went to the public showers once a week on Saturday mornings. I joined Salomon when I was nine. In all weather, we stood in line outside the building, on the sidewalk, usually for an hour. We had fifteen minutes to take the shower. We were happy to feel clean and to smell relatively good, thanks to the soap called "savon de Marseille," a popular brand that was also used to wash clothes. The public baths were relatively expensive and always busy. We could afford them only once a week. That was the only day of the week when we put on clean underwear and a clean shirt!

Our grandmother, "Boubé," was mean; probably embittered by the suffering she had endured most of her life. In her youth in Poland she had known dire poverty and the fear of the pogroms. As a married woman, she had lost her husband to typhus at the age of thirty leaving her with eight children to care for. During World War II, four of her sons were exterminated. She showed us no compassion. She never exhibited any love or affection toward us. She was severely afflicted with painful rheumatism. There were no painkillers then. She often asked Salomon and me to urinate into a basin in which she would then dip her deformed hands. She swore that it lessened the constant pain. Like the children we were, we would laugh. She only spoke Yiddish and Polish. The only normal conversations she had were with her daughter Sarah, our Aunt. She had a grudge against her son-in-law, Uncle Charles. We never knew the reason. During the four years I stayed in that home I never heard them speak to each other. For no reason at all, maybe due to some dementia, she would abuse Salomon with vulgarities, in Yiddish, a language rich with such expressions.

I never stopped voicing my unhappiness during my stay there. I had hoped that showing my contempt would make them realize that they had made a mistake in separating us from the Ribouleau family. They seemed to have no understanding, no remorse, no compassion for our loss.

Is it possible that they were interested in the financial gain that we brought as war orphans and children of deportees? Or by our parents' furniture which they quickly moved from the apartment in Compiègne to St Quentin? It did not amount to much, but after the war everything was valuable. They had collected Salomon's mother's furniture, which his mother's Aunt had preciously stored for the duration of the war. They also benefited from my sister's labor.

Uncle Charles and Aunt Sarah did not know the meaning of

the words "affection" or "love." These feelings were totally foreign to them.

Both worked hard. Rain, shine, or snow they left, almost every day, at 5:30 a.m. for the markets where they installed their stand and unloaded about a thousand pounds of clothes, repacked them in the early afternoon, and returned around two or three o'clock. Tired from a hard day, they came home to an atmosphere of rebellion. Salomon and I did everything possible to make their life miserable. Rachel had given up the fight. She wanted peace.

Salomon was very unhappy there as well. His father Meyer died in 1937 due to complications after an ulcer surgery. With Salomon just eighteen months old, his mother Aunt Gela was left destitute. She had no means of subsistence, and to avoid losing her son to starvation or sickness she was forced to place him with the OSE organization at the beginning of the war.

Salomon spent close to six years with OSE, hidden and protected by this wonderful humanitarian organization. To avoid detection and capture by the Nazis, he was moved many times from orphanages to private homes with courageous people who were willing to risk their lives to save the lives of innocent and persecuted children. He was happy living with the many children who surrounded him. He never felt threatened except for one difficult and dangerous incident. The SS raided an orphanage in the town of Lourdes, where Salomon was, suspecting or informed that Jewish children were there. They ordered all the boys to line up and drop their pants in front of a French doctor who had been ordered to set aside the boys who were circumcised. When Sali's turn came the SS man overlooking the doctor was called away. Although Sali was circumcised the doctor told him to put his pants back on and move on. That good doctor saved Sali's life and could have lost his own that day.

Sali was brought to the Blum family in December 1945, thinking that he was coming for a few days. He had a head full of beautiful red hair, which was the subject of mockery by the family and his school peers. He suffered from nocturnal urinary incontinence, which probably could have been cured if he had been allowed to see a doctor. Every night the bed sheets were drenched. Aunt Sarah, Uncle Charles, and "Boubé," assuming that he was doing this on purpose, castigated him to no end. I was sharing his bed. It was far from being comfortable! I felt very bad for him. He was always nice to me.

*Leon and Rachel 1948*

Each evening, before falling asleep, my despair would hit me hard. Salomon comforted me with words of hope.

He had a great Aunt, his mother's Aunt, who lived around the corner from us. Aunt Rachel, as we called her, was a wonderful person. Salomon loved her. He had lunch with her every Sunday. He would go and visit with her sometimes during the week. There, he found for a few hours, a haven of love and affection he, like me, craved for. Unfortunately for all, our uncle and aunt did not know how to dispense any. I envied him for he was able to see, every week, someone who loved him. From time to time I accompanied him. Aunt Rachel lived on the second floor of an old attached building. We would race up the stairs. She opened the door with a smile on her tired face. Her little apartment smelled of baking and wax. It was so clean we could eat on the floor. Despite her poverty, she always had something sweet cooking for us and most importantly she gave us kindness and comfort.

While we were still with the Ribouleau family, my sister Rachel attended a secretarial school. When we arrived in Saint-Quentin, she could easily have found a position as a secretary. Instead, she became the domestic of the family. She did the house cleaning, the laundry, the ironing, and some cooking. In addition, every morning, she went with Uncle and Aunt to the open markets. She did it all and never complained.

After I succeeded in graduating earlier from primary school when I was twelve, I was admitted to the Lycée (high school). My uncle and aunt argued that the education would be too expensive and they needed me to work with them on the open markets. Rachel told them that her work, which she was not paid for, should take care of my schooling expenses.

Shortly after I started to attend the Lycée, I was confronted with heartbreaking news: Rachel was to emigrate to the United States. Among the many concerns about this shocking news, Rachel was worried that I would be pulled out of school as soon as she left. She went to see my school principal, explained the situation, and paid for my expenses a year in advance with money that Papa and Maman Ribouleau had sent to her.

She thought that within a year, I would be reunited with her in the USA.

# Chapter 19

# Another Separation

Soon after the war ended, Uncle Charles went to the United States to visit his sister Rose in New York. He had not seen her for more than twenty years, since she had emigrated from Poland in the 1920s. About two years later, he made a second trip. When he came back, he and Aunt Sarah pulled Rachel in the living room, closed the door and told her "You are going to America as soon as you receive your visa and a passport. You are going to live with my sister Rose and her family."

Rachel was totally unprepared for the news. She turned pale and anxiously asked "What about Leon?"

"He will join you later. Aunt Rose and her husband, Max, have room for only one person at this time. They already have three children," Uncle Charles said without seeming to understand the turmoil he was causing.

Guessing that an important event would be discussed, my cousin Salomon and I had one ear glued to the door. We heard the entire conversation. I opened the door and rushed into the living room and yelled pleading "Rachel, no, please, I do not want you to leave! I am miserable here. I cannot stay without you."

"We are not asking you for your opinion! You are only a child," screamed Aunt Sarah.

She had straightened up to tower over me, and I thought she was going to hit me. She looked at me with contempt. It has been so many years, and I still see the scene. It was a life-changing moment.

I did not know how monumental of an upheaval it would be.

"Rachel is going to America!" She said firmly.

"You are not going to separate me from my sister," I yelled. "She is the only person in this house who cares about me. You have already separated me once from the people I love."

Rachel was overwhelmed with emotion and she could not

speak. She came to me and held me tight. I was reliving the nightmare of when our parents were taken away by the gendarmes. How can adults be so cruel and insensitive to the pain and grief of a twelve-year-old child?

"I will not let you do that to us," I shouted.

"Leon, please calm down." Rachel pleaded.

There was no changing their minds. Once more, adults decided my fate. Rachel did not have much of a choice. She was hardly sixteen. The legal age was twenty-one. What could she say? The room was filled with anguish. This home had never seen happy moments, and the next six months until Rachel's departure were dreadful.

To give me some solace and hope, Rachel kept telling me, "You will come and join me very soon. I will work and save to pay for your trip to America."

"What is going to happen to me without your protection? I cannot stay here any longer. They hate me." I told her.

I was tormented by the thought of the upcoming separation. I would toss and turn in the bed I was still sharing with my cousin Salomon. I kept him awake, as well. He was the only one in the family besides my sister who tried to give me some consolation.

Rachel attempted a number of times to convince our uncle and aunt not to separate us. She insisted that we should go to America together.

"Let me stay here. I will work even harder. I will save to pay for the cost of the trip for both of us," she pleaded. "I cannot abandon Leon. We have already lost our parents. He has been separated from the people he considered his father and mother. He has been miserable in this house. He will never get used to living with you, especially without me. I must stay until we can leave together," Rachel implored.

They held their ground showing no compassion.

"All this is childishness. Rachel, you will thank us one day. You are going," replied Aunt Sarah.

In order to obtain an immigration visa, my sister needed to undergo a physical. As she was very skinny, she hoped that she would fail. Against her wishes she passed the physical. The visa arrived shortly thereafter. I was becoming more hostile and more aggressive as the departure day was approaching.

"You are not any better than the *boches!*" I screamed at them desperately.

It was difficult to hold back my resentment. I swore silently to seek revenge for the pain this family inflicted on me. They had abruptly separated me from the Ribouleau family and forced me to live in a home devoid of affection. My sister was my only support, my only hope for a better life. She continued to be like a mother to me. She was the only person I could talk to and trust, with the exception of my cousin Salomon, who was himself mistreated even worse than I was.

During the German occupation, I lived with fear. In Saint-Quentin, the fear had been replaced with anger, discouragement, and a sense of great injustice.

"You will see Rachel again soon," Salomon would tell me reassuringly. "It's only a question of a few months. As for me, I am condemned to stay in that damn house!"

"I do not know what I will do without her, Salomon. I just cannot get used to the idea," I would respond.

The day of departure was drawing close. My anxiety was such that I could no longer communicate with anyone, even with my sister. I realized that I was putting a heavy burden on her shoulders, but I was incapable of normalcy. I was mad at the whole world. She would look at me with her big and sad eyes, attempting to engage into a conversation. She had stopped trying to reassure me that we would be together again soon.

I was reliving the nightmare of July 19, 1942. This time, my own family was responsible for this cruel separation.

I was not even allowed to accompany my sister to Cherbourg, the town where she was to board the ship that would take her to America, a new country she had never been to and a new family she had never met.

It was a cold day in December 1949. Rachel was wearing a heavy gray coat that she had bought with money the Ribouleau family had sent her. Our uncle and aunt had refused to buy her any clothes for this trip, claiming that in America the family would buy her all the clothes she needed.

We hugged each other, tears blinding us.

"Be courageous, Leon. We will soon be reunited. I will write to you as soon as I arrive. Please write to me often. I need to hear from you," she told me anxiously.

"Rachel …" I stammered. Grief was choking me. I was not able to speak.

Uncle Blum looked annoyed. He did not show any emotion. He kept urging my sister to board the train, probably afraid that she would change her mind.

In those days, one needed to purchase a ticket to gain access to the railroad platform. Uncle and Aunt Blum had refused to buy our cousin Salomon one. They said it was too costly. He was sad not to be able to accompany Rachel to the train. He was playing with the dispensing machine. Miracle! Without putting any coin in, a ticket came out! He ran to the platform and was able to be with us and to see Rachel for a few minutes before she disappeared.

Our cousin Jean Gerbaez, in his mid-twenties, had been entrusted to accompany my sister to Cherbourg, where the Queen Mary I, an English ship, was docked and would be taking Rachel to America. Cherbourg was about six hours away from Saint-Quentin by rail. It was Jean's mother, our Aunt Ida, who had changed our destiny when she failed to testify in our behalf as planned at the Family Council.

The return home was like coming back from a funeral. It was very difficult to restrain myself from howling my grief. I was on the verge of madness. I wanted to beat my uncle and aunt. I could never forgive them. I hated them as much as I hated the Germans who had murdered my parents.

I was twelve years old. I did not know at the time that I would not see my sister or hear her voice for the next fourteen years.

Rachel boarded the Queen Mary I on December 10, 1949. She was extremely distraught to leave without me. She felt like a mother abandoning her child. Since our parents were taken away, she had filled the void and taken on their role. The voyage was dreadful. She could not stop crying and thought a number of times of jumping overboard to stop the pain and end the nightmare. In addition, the winter crossing was very trying. She was seasick most of the time. She felt so lonely, lost despite the fact that there were over one thousand passengers around her. Most of them only spoke English, which she did not understand at all. A group of young Jewish men from Romania, noticing how miserable Rachel was, engaged her in conversation. They communicated in Yiddish, a language that Rachel and I had learned while we stayed in Saint-Quentin. She, at last, had someone to talk to. This encounter helped dull her pain and may have saved her life.

Aunt Rose, our mother's sister and her husband Uncle Max Rosenblum were happy to welcome this unknown niece, a survivor of their own family devastated by the Nazis. At the arrival of the Queen Mary I in New York harbor, although they had photos of Rachel, they were concerned to miss her among the thousand passengers who were disembarking. Rachel had cut her long hair short and was afraid they might not recognize her! They had made a big sign with her name on it. Eventually they found each other.

The Rosenblum family lived in Brooklyn. Aunt Rose, Uncle Max, their son Irving, and two daughters, Shirley, already married, and Eileen, eleven years old, welcomed her warmly. The first months were extremely difficult for Rachel. Outside of the house, people spoke English. No one spoke French in the family or in the circle of friends. Fortunately, she was able to communicate with the family and acquaintances in Yiddish, a language spoken in those days in almost every Jewish home, as most parents were of the first generation of immigrants.

She could not shake the sadness of leaving me. Nothing was familiar here. Her loneliness was overwhelming, although the family was trying very hard to make her feel at home.

"You will quickly get accustomed to America; you are going to love it here," repeated Aunt Rose to Rachel, trying to help her to get out of her depression.

"When can Leon come and join me?" my sister was constantly asking.

"It is not possible now. Our apartment is too small for all of us already. We are not earning enough to take care of your brother. We are probably not even meeting the government guaranty requirements to obtain a visa for Leon."

My sister sent me letters often. She told me a number of times that she intended to return to France. This was a practical impossibility. She felt so guilty to have left me behind.

Rachel was eager to earn money, so that she could meet the government requirements and bring me over or enable her to return to France, and she turned down my Aunt Rose and Uncle Max's generous offer to fund her education. Rachel's sadness was weighing heavily on the family.

Rachel took a job at the hat factory where Uncle Max was employed. This manufacturing job did not require language skills.

Saving to bring me over had become an obsession and her main objective in life.

The first evening after Rachel arrived in New York, Izzy, a handsome young man, nineteen years old, came to the house after dinner to meet the young girl everyone in the neighborhood had been talking about for months. He was working, at the time, for our cousin Irving, who owned a TV repair shop. The family had shown Izzy pictures of a smiling Rachel, and he had found her beautiful and had fallen in love with the girl in the photos. When he met her in person, however, she did not look quite like the pictures. She was very tired from the difficult Atlantic crossing. She looked sad. She hardly paid attention to him and showed no interest in engaging in a conversation. She was sitting at the kitchen table writing me a letter. He felt pity for her. Despite this cool first day reception, he came back every evening after dinner to see her. They spoke Yiddish to each other. Rachel shared with him her distress. She was obsessed with my situation.

"How do we bring my brother over?" she kept asking.

Izzy's family lived from paycheck to paycheck. They could not help. All shared her pain and tried to comfort her as best they could.

Izzy started to teach her English. He took her to the Coney Island amusement park. He was very proud of the used Model "A" Ford he had recently bought for sixty dollars. He was also very proud of the very beautiful girl sitting next to him in his shiny blue and black convertible. They saw each other every day. My sister was discovering America, more precisely the New York area, and more importantly the happiness of being in love and being loved. She could see the possibility of starting her own family and not depending on someone else for the first time in her life.

On her birthday, April 29, 1950, Izzy offered her a necklace with a golden medallion, beautifully engraved with a Star of David on the cover and a place for a photo inside.

"Izzy, let's get married!" she bluntly told him to his great surprise.

"I am only nineteen years old. I only make fifteen dollars a week. How would we pay for the rent and the food?" he asked her.

"However," he added, "if you can find a place to live that we can afford on our income, yes, we will get married."

Tears of joy streaming down her happy face, she was convinced that she would succeed in finding such a place, soon.

"Two can live almost as cheap as one," she told him. When we are married, we can start the process to bring Leon over. Right?" she asked enthusiastically.

She still was distressed over our separation.

Due to a business slowdown, Izzy had to find another job. He managed to get one almost immediately with a substantial salary increase, twice what he was making. Thirty dollars a week was in these days considered a decent salary. Between Izzy and Rachel's income, they could afford to get married, feed themselves, pay a modest rent, and save money.

They were married on December 24, 1950, a year and nine days after Rachel set foot on American soil. They rented a room in the home of an older lady, who was so delighted to have this young couple in her home that she only charged them half the going rental price.

Four months later, Rachel was pregnant. In her seventh month of pregnancy, Izzy was asked to report to the Armed Services. The United States was at war with North Korea. Due to Rachel's pregnancy, he was exempted from duty. Anita was born January 19, 1952. Shortly thereafter, they undertook the task of preparing the paperwork to bring me over. Disappointment, again. Immigration turned down the request on the grounds that their income was too low.

After my sister's departure, I sank into deep despair. My anger was intense. I needed to express it, one way or another. I refused categorically to go and help on the markets, Thursdays and Saturdays, as they had forced me to do in the last couple of years. I no longer could concentrate on my studies. I had lost interest and self-discipline. One of the professors asked to meet with me. I had gone from being a good to a mediocre student. He knew that I had lost my parents to the Holocaust and that I was living with an aunt and uncle. He guessed that I had family problems and showed understanding. He expressed his concern.

"Think of your future, Malmed. You are compromising it. Let us help you." he said with compassion.

I shut myself off. I could not respond to this kind and wise person without coming apart. I did not want to break down in front of him. I missed an opportunity that set me back one or two years. I shrugged my shoulders. I could not answer his questions. I was not able, emotionally, to share with him the desperation, the suffering, and the isolation I felt. I could not understand why fate was repeatedly separating me from those I loved and who loved me.

After school, instead of going to a home that I loathed, I would meet friends my age at the local "café" and play fuss-ball.

My cousin Sali and I were so full of anger at the repression and the lack of love that we looked for mischief. We tried to make cigarettes using dry grass that we found on empty lots and that looked like tobacco leaves but were not—far from it. When we took a few puffs from these home-made cigarettes both of us became very sick. When we had some money, we would buy English cigarettes, called Craven. They came in packs of five; that was all we could afford.

About a year after my sister's departure, my cousin, Salomon, was thrown out of the house for some benign remark he had made. He was fifteen years old. With the help of the Jewish community of Saint-Quentin, he was able to continue his studies at a vocational school, where he earned a degree in machine tools operation. Without Salomon, I felt even more isolated. I had no one to talk to. I would vent my anger and loneliness in letters to my sister and to my dear Ribouleau family. It was my only outlet.

Pushed to the breaking point, I needed to do something to get out of the trap I felt I was in. But what? How?

No one in my immediate surroundings could help me out of the quicksand I was fast sinking in. The kind letters that Rachel wrote were no longer sufficient to keep me quiet.

I decided to speak to my Aunt and Uncle. Each evening, I would say:

"I want to go back to Compiègne."

"What! Are you crazy? Never!" Uncle Charles would yell.

Each day, I welcomed them with the same request. Those were the only words I would exchange with them. Aunt Sarah would scream obscenities at me in Yiddish. My parents had been taken away from me. I was separated from a family I had fallen in love with and who loved me. My sister, a second mother to me, was forced against her will to go and live 4,000 miles away. Who did I have left? Except for my cousin Salomon who was not here any longer, there was no one who could give me a semblance of love, of affection, of comprehension.

"I am their prisoner," I would complain to Salomon when we met on Sundays "They cannot keep me against my will. I am going to escape."

I would write long letters to Papa and Maman Ribouleau. They were powerless. They assured me that I would always be welcome in their home but they could not intervene without breaking the law. Legally, they could not entice me to leave.

"We are going to send you to an orphanage," Aunt Blum said, her face distorted with anger. They meant it.

"I will run away," I answered. "Why don't you let me go back to Compiègne?" I asked.

One day, I thought of contacting the president of the Jewish community of Saint-Quentin. It took me a week to build up the courage to walk to his store and ask him if I could talk to him about family matters. Monsieur Zilberberg, a kind and intelligent person, who inspired trust, asked me what this was about. I explained my situation and I concluded for him:

"My sister left for America two years ago. She has not been able to bring me over as planned. I want to return to the Ribouleau family. They love me. I love them. They are my second parents. They risked their lives and their sons' lives to save ours. They are willing to take me back. Please help me. I cannot stay any longer with my uncle and aunt. They want to send me to an orphanage. The situation is affecting my sanity. I do not know what to do any longer."

"Listen Leon, be patient," he told me. "I give you my word that I will discuss the situation with my colleagues. We will find a solution to your problem. Please do not do anything foolish in the mean time."

He kept his word. A few weeks later, he asked Uncle and Aunt to attend a meeting. I was told they were surprised and angry at me for bringing this issue to the community. They did not know that I had contacted Mr. Zilberberg.

He told them: "This boy is thirteen years old. He is a mature teenager. He is very unhappy and has been since you brought him to your home. Put yourselves in his shoes. Why would you keep insisting that he stays with you? You are all extremely unhappy. My colleagues and I strongly recommend that you let him go back to the Ribouleau family. That is where he wants to live. You have fulfilled your duty to his parents, your brother and sister."

That same evening, they told me that I was free to leave.

A huge wave of happiness came over me and left me speechless. I wanted to jump over roofs.

For the first time in four years, I felt free.

Chapter 20

# The "Gendarmes"

While I lived in Saint-Quentin, close to four years, I was allowed to come back to Compiègne during school holidays. I looked forward to these stays with great excitement. However, I dreaded the thought of having to return to Saint-Quentin at the end of these precious times. Whenever I came back to Compiègne I was welcomed with open arms. Papa Henri and Maman Suzanne treated me like their son. It was like coming back from a school internship. The days I stayed with them were numbered and went by quickly. I practically jumped off the train when it slowed down at the Compiègne train station. Papa and Maman Ribouleau waited for me on the train platform. We would kiss and say very little, holding our emotions. While I was away for months at a time, I was disciplined and wrote to them every other week. When we were together I tried not to burden them with my miserable life in Saint-Quentin. They knew how unhappy I was there. I wanted the three of us to enjoy the moments we had together.

At the end of the war, the French Armed Forces had been dismantled and were practically nonexistent. The Germans had stolen the French treasury. The organization called "Les Aréostiers," where papa and maman Ribouleau had been employed for many years was shut down. They were out of a job with six people to feed; unemployment benefits did not exist in those days. Papa Henri's specialty, rope making, was no longer useful since cars had replaced horses, airplanes had replaced hot air balloons, and machinery had replaced manual rope making. They remembered our father encouraging them, before he was deported, to work for themselves. He had promised that he would help them if they ever decided to change careers.

They contacted Joseph Epelberg, the very close friend of our parents and the same Joseph who courted my mother in the early 1930s and whom my father had chased away. Joseph and his wife Suzanne loved Rachel and me. They had escaped the Holocaust. Joseph had been able to get his wife and his daughter out of the Vel d'Hiv' round-up by bribing a French policeman with a fur coat and cash. Both were extremely sad to have lost their friends, our parents. They were in awe of what the Ribouleaus had done for us. He wanted to pay them back and help. He encouraged them to follow my father's advice. He introduced them to a few of my father's suppliers who had survived the war. Joseph told them that they had saved our lives and had even paid the rent the last three years so that our parents would have their apartment when they came back. The suppliers gave Papa Henri all the merchandise they needed at the lowest cost possible, on consignment, to get started. Papa Henri and Maman Suzanne were able to get their little enterprise going with practically no cash. They paid the suppliers whenever the merchandise was sold.

More suppliers joined in as they learned what the Ribouleau family had done for a Jewish family. Papa and Maman Ribouleau were able to take advantage of those very generous financial terms for a number of years. They did not have a storefront. They worked on the open markets, the same way our parents had made their living. Was there continuity? Was there some kind of a thread between the Ribouleau and the Malmed families?

Papa Henri started his business career using a small trailer—the same trailer that my sister and I used to sit in when we went on fishing expeditions at the lakes "Etangs de Saint-Pierre." He pulled the trailer loaded with merchandise behind his bicycle to the markets in the surrounding towns four to twenty miles away, rain or shine, six days a week.

After about a year he bought his first car, a "Chenard and Walker." He had it modified into a small van by a craftsman who used to build and repair horse carriages. A few cars later he bought a van specifically designed for transport. It was manufactured by Renault and nicknamed a "Mille kilogs" because it was capable of carrying two thousand pounds. Most people in the trade used such vans. They came in one color: grey. By then Papa and Maman Ribouleau sold men's clothing. They had a following of loyal customers and they made a good living.

It was hard work. Six days a week they unloaded close to two thousand pounds in the morning and reloaded in early afternoon or evening. On Mondays, they went to Paris to buy merchandise.

The merchandise was displayed on a relatively light structure that needed to be assembled and dismantled every day. It consisted of steel tubes and a roof made of waterproof canvas to protect the merchandise against the rain and the sun. In winter, it was particularly difficult to handle the tubes with gloves. Most of the time we did not wear any. The bare fingers would stick to the freezing steel tubes. The merchandise had to be carried from the van to the tabletop and be arranged attractively.

When I came to Compiègne during school vacations, Maman Suzanne stayed home. I went with Papa Henri instead and helped him out with the set up, selling, and the repacking. When I was thirteen or fourteen, he let me drive the truck. The pedals were out of reach. He fabricated two pieces of wood that he attached to the pedals so that I could reach. I was happy to help out. It felt so much like home when I was in Compiègne. In addition, I loved my hometown and its surrounding forest. I knew so many people. The neighbors would often come over and talk. They would ask about my sister and me. "Leon, you are almost a man now! How are you? How do you like living in Saint-Quentin? Do you miss Compiègne? How is your sister doing? Do you hear from her?"

I was about thirteen at the time. I never talked about my difficult situation in Saint-Quentin. I was still embarrassed when people showed pity. The expression "poor child" that I heard once in a while, though heartfelt, bothered me.

One Thursday morning, Papa Henri and I attended the market of Verberie, a small town about fifteen miles away from Compiègne. I was behind the stall waiting for customers. As every morning, we had gotten up early; I was bored and yawning. Papa Henri was busy talking to two "gendarmes" in front of the stall. I had never seen them around. I noticed that every so often, the three of them would turn around to look in my direction. I thought that they may be talking about my yawning. However, they were not smiling. Maybe Papa Henri was telling them the sad events of the war. They probably felt bad about what had happened to our parents. Papa Henri looked at me and motioned me to come and join them. I looked at him questioningly, as I did not care to talk to any gendarmes.

"Leon, come around and say hello to these people," he said.

I went under the stall to avoid a longer walk around and joined the small group. Both "gendarmes" were looking at me strangely.

They seemed embarrassed, out of place. Did I do anything wrong? I could not remember if I did or not. They seemed tall and threatening in their uniforms. Were they sweating? It was not that hot. One of them cleared his throat and said:

"Come on, my boy, let's shake hands."

I started to raise my hand when papa Henri said calmly:

"These are the gendarmes who ..."

Before he ended the sentence, I knew who they were. I had a flashback. I froze, horrified.

I was transported, to July 19, 1942. I could see the scene: my mother in tears, my father pulling his hair and these "two gendarmes," in maybe the same uniforms they wore today, ordering my parents to hurry up while my sister Rachel and I were clinging at our mother's dress.

It seemed that a long time passed and my arm was still half way up. Was it five seconds, ten? A minute, two minutes? I could not tell. I was looking at the people who sent my parents to their death. I was staring hatefully at this man I was about to shake hands with. I was paralyzed. I did not know what to do. Should I spit at their faces? Should I pound them with my fists? Should I tell them how much I hated them? Should I insult them and humiliate them in front of all? Should I ask them why they collaborated, and sent my parents to die? I could not speak. I could not move. I felt the rage taking over. I was trying hard to repress it. I knew that if I said anything I would not be able to hold my tears. I did not want to cry in front of these monsters, these traitors. I hated them like I have never hated anyone like this before.

I did not understand why Papa Henri had put me in such a position. How could he think that I wanted to shake hands and talk with such people? Sixty years later, I may be able to talk to them but I would never shake their hands, never.

Abruptly, I turned my back to them and walked away. I walked the streets of Verberie for several hours. I had no idea where I was going or even where I was. It did not matter. I was full of anger and resentment. I could not understand that they were still in their uniforms when they should be in jail. They had committed treason for obeying enemy orders. These two gendarmes and many of their colleagues throughout France collaborated and helped the Nazis murder more than seventy thousand innocents.

*Were they intelligent enough to understand the crimes they committed? Could they feel the anguish of the families of the innocents they handed over to the German Nazis and the never-ending pain that I carried then and continue to carry. No, I could never forgive them.*

I had to come back, though, to help Papa Henri pack up. I wanted to speak to him about what had happened. At the same time, I did not want to embarrass him. He did not say anything. He looked sad, embarrassed, agitated. Strangely, we never talked about this event.

I never saw these "gendarmes" again. I am sure they avoided the Verberie market on Thursdays.

*Did anyone ask them why they had collaborated? Why they submitted so easily, without any resistance to the Nazis? Did they sleep well at night? Did they ever share with their spouses, their children, their friends any remorse for their participation in the heinous crimes committed, or did they try to justify their lack of courage?*

After the war, as far as I know, none of the people employed in the different French administrations who collaborated with the enemy were ever questioned and punished. With their blind obedience to the monstrous invaders, they contributed directly to send ten of thousands of innocent people to jails, internment and deportation camps where they were tortured, enslaved, and murdered.

Were they afraid to lose their jobs? Could they have forewarned the people they were told to arrest? Of course they could have. Those "gendarmes" knew my parents well. Our father helped them many number of times by tailoring their uniforms at no charge. Their cowardice and selfishness drove them to blindly join forces with the enemy.

When I am in France visiting, it is difficult to see a "gendarme" without thinking about their predecessors, their fathers or grandfathers who collaborated with the enemy during World War II. I wonder if these keepers of the law, these people that we put our trust in to keep us safe would act the same way should they be faced with the same situation today?

The fact that no action was ever taken with these collaborators is a sad example for the future generations of law enforcement officers. It has left me and many others with a deep feeling of injustice for the many that suffered and died because of the cowardice of government employees.

On July 16, 1995, after five decades of silence by the French elected officials, President Jacques Chirac, courageously recognized publicly France's responsibility for the deportation of over seventy thousand Jews to their deaths during World War II. He said:

> *These dark hours stain forever our history and are an insult to our past and our traditions. Yes, the criminal madness of the occupant was, we all know, assisted by French citizens, assisted by the French government. France, motherland of the Lights, motherland of the Human Rights, land of sanctuary for many, land of haven, France on that day performed the irreparable.*

In July of 2012 at a commemoration of the 70th anniversary of the two-day police roundup of more than 13,000 Jews in Paris in July 1942 (commonly referred to as "the Vel' d'hiv round-up"), and following in the footsteps of former president Jacques Chirac, newly elected President François Hollande said that France bore responsibility for the killings of thousands of Jewish people who were detained and deported to Nazi concentration camps during World War Two. He said:

> *The truth is that this was a crime against France, a betrayal of her values; the same values the Resistance, the Free French, the Just embodied with honor.*

Papa Henri was very respectful of the authorities. I suppose that these two "gendarmes" wanted to shake my hand to make them feel good and to erase the past as if this simple gesture was sufficient to be forgiven and to heal the wounds. Papa Henri did not want to hurt their feelings and probably did not want to have problems with the police in general. He thought he was doing the right thing. I regret not having discussed this painful encounter with him afterwards. Again we wanted to put the past behind us. I did not want to upset the profound love I felt towards Papa Henri and Maman Suzanne. I cherished them and would never forget that they saved my life. They probably thought that I needed to move forward, not to let the past hold me back and not to let the pain of the memories hold me prisoner. I wanted to forget as well. Strong emotions would surface whenever a conversation about the war events was started.

I had decided to close the door on the past. I locked that door and threw the key as far away as possible, hoping I would never find it.

Sixty years later, I realized that time never healed my injuries. I was still hurting. I had to revisit the torment of those horrible years.

I have been told that after completing this book, I would feel better. I would be able to speak freely about these difficult years. I am not convinced I will ever heal. I wished I had undertaken the writing of this book earlier. I would have liked so much for Papa Henri, Maman Suzanne, René, and Marcel to read about the love and the respect my sister and I have for them. They are no longer here to answer the many questions I never dared ask and that will never be answered.

The encounter with the gendarmes did not tarnish my relationship with Papa Henri. We came back home from Verberie that day, both of us kind of stunned by the incident. I do not know if he ever talked to Maman Suzanne about it. I suppose he did. She never brought it up with me. Some seventy years later, it appears simple. It was not then.

For the remainder of the vacation, I continued to go with Papa Henri to the markets. Every time, I saw a "gendarme," my heart rate accelerated. The end of my vacations approached, the thought of returning to Saint-Quentin for another four to five months was traumatizing.

I dreaded the separations from them and these comfortable surroundings. Papa Henri and Maman Suzanne accompanied me to the train station. I embraced them and boarded the train very distressed. I kept my forehead glued to the window until I could not see them anymore. Next vacation I would be coming back and be happy again. The love that they showed my sister and me was always so welcome.

"Come back soon," Maman Suzanne had told me before departing. "Our home is yours."

Chapter 21

# Back in Compiègne

Soon after I was told that I was free to return to Compiègne, I left Saint-Quentin on the first day of school vacation, in July 1953. This time, I had no return train ticket. It was taking me to where I wanted to live. I did not have to dread having to go back. My heart was pounding when I saw Papa Henri and Maman Suzanne. I was apprehensive and insecure.

Both were smiling radiantly. I ran into their arms dragging my suitcase with the few clothes and mementos I had piled up before leaving Saint-Quentin behind forever. I had been hoping and waiting for this moment for a long time.

I felt a ping of guilt thinking of my cousin Salomon in his miserable hotel room. He had been my brother, my family, my friend, my support during those four years of unhappiness and despair.

I was fourteen years old. Since Rachel had left, I had transitioned from childhood to adulthood. The challenges of the last ten years had made me suspicious of adults and I was determined to be as independent as possible.

I loved Papa Henri and Maman Suzanne and I knew that it was reciprocal.

I remained concerned. *Would they keep me? Would they get tired of having another person in their home? Why would they bother with me? Their sons were married. They were enjoying a good life after raising René, Marcel, Rachel, and me during three years of famine and mortal danger.*

Looking at the family pictures in my new bedroom, the pictures of René and Marcel brought back fond memories. René Ribouleau and Cécile looked so happy. Their love endured the rest of their life. Marcel Ribouleau had met Gilberte, his future wife at a Youth meeting. She worked for Dr. Kaufman who had miraculously escaped deportation and extermination. Dr. Kaufman was a general practitioner with an excellent reputation as a good doctor and a very charitable person. The Germans requisitioned his large home-office shortly after the occupation began. He was given a few hours to move out his personal belongings but had to leave all his furniture in place.

A couple of years after Rachel and I went to live in Saint-Quentin, Papa Henri and Maman Suzanne had moved from 17 rue St Fiacre to a beautiful villa on the "rue St Joseph" two to three miles away. The home was set back from the sidewalk. In front of the house was a flowerbed filled with colorful flowers well maintained by Papa Henri. Hanging from the upstairs bedroom windowsill was a long flower pot full of geraniums. The Ribouleaus won the annual contest for the best decorated home of Compiègne four years in a row.

My room was a far cry from the windowless closet I had been sleeping in during my stay in Saint-Quentin. It seemed immense! There was a large desk where I would be doing my homework instead of a corner of a dining room table with people constantly milling around. I had a bathroom to myself! I could not believe that it was possible to have so much comfort. I had only known the accommodations of Saint-Quentin, where eight of us—three adults and five children—lived in a minuscule home. I was now swimming in luxury. This home was calm, something I was not used to. Most important, I was with people who loved me and made me feel welcome, something I was not used to either.

Sensing my intense emotion, Papa Henri said: "Come on, Leon, the bad days are over. You are home again. You have nothing to fear here. Come and have a snack."

Maman Suzanne added, "I baked a pie you like with cherries from our garden."

With these simple words the last, long and difficult four years seemed to fade away for the moment. We all sat down at the kitchen table and enjoyed the delicious treat.

The house at 82 rue Saint Joseph was a two-story structure. A dog, a "Bouvier des Flandres," originally bred as a herding dog, named Yolti, was trained to bring us our respective slippers when we came in the house. We smiled and laughed each time she did that. The kitchen, forever smelling good, was on the left of the entryway and the dining room on the right. Papa Henri and Maman Suzanne's bedroom was off the kitchen. In the middle of the hallway was a door leading to the stairs and to the two bedrooms on the second floor.

I opened my suitcase and set up a photo of my parents and one of Rachel on the night table. The large window had a view on the garden where Papa Henri grew vegetables, fruits, and flowers. In the middle of the garden was a cherry tree that produced year after year in abundance. Between the kitchen and the garden was a veranda with a birdcage and several canaries singing most of the time. This house was a haven of happiness compared to where I came from!

Still, I had to make difficult adjustments. After Rachel left Saint-Quentin for the USA I had picked up bad habits. I started to smoke, only a few cigarettes a day but it still was difficult to stop. After school I used to go to the "café-bar" and play fuss-ball instead of going home and doing my homework. Coming back to Compiègne I had committed myself to clean up and take advantage of the opportunity that was offered and start on a good foot. I threw away the few cigarettes I had left.

I wanted to minimize the burden on Papa and Maman Ribouleau. I volunteered to help at the markets on my days off from school, Thursdays, Saturday afternoons, and Sundays. On Thursdays and Sundays, we left home at seven in the morning and came back around two in the afternoon. On Saturdays, we also left early but came home at about seven in the evening, as the market lasted all day. They were long days. These activities did not leave me with much time to study and play. I also helped with the garden. It required daily care. I learned very early about home maintenance and masonry. We built a wall around the property. I was still concerned that I did not do enough for them. I was so grateful to be here that I wanted to do everything possible to please Papa Henri and Maman Suzanne.

The events of the last ten years had been so unsettling that I had lost the notion of security, even with this loving family. I was afraid they would tire of me and ask me to go back to Saint-Quentin or somewhere else. I was still haunted by Uncle and Aunt Blum's threat to send me to an orphanage.

But Papa Henri and Maman Suzanne were never anything but kind and loving toward me. Maman Suzanne would help me select my clothes. She even recommended that I get my clothes tailor-made. Even though she was raised in a very poor environment and with very little education, she had developed a very good taste for clothes, furniture, art, cooking and more. I was equally comfortable with Papa Henri. Once or twice a week, the two of us, sometimes Marcel would join us, went fishing. We had the opportunity to talk about anything and everything. Maman Suzanne, probably due to menopause, occasionally would become angry at the slightest annoyance. Her anger was always directed toward Papa Henri. I felt somehow responsible and I quickly left the room and took refuge in my bedroom hoping that the storm would blow away.

Between school and helping, I did not have time to go out with friends of my age, except for some Sunday afternoons I went to a movie with a schoolmate who lived close by.

Integration into a new school proved difficult. I transferred from Saint-Quentin to a high school in Compiègne. The teachers' lack of discipline and interest in the behavior of the students were in stark contrast with the Saint-Quentin high school. Students of all ages were allowed to smoke in the playground. It was night and day compared with the school I came from. After a wasted year, I enrolled in a different school with an excellent reputation. It was a good move that changed the course of my education and my life. The principal "Monsieur" Gibereau, who taught math, was my best teacher ever. Every Thursday, a day off for all schools, he tutored me, refusing to be paid. He helped me tremendously, and for the first time in my life, I understood what I was doing and felt comfortable. I was no longer afraid of mathematics. Unfortunately, I never had the opportunity as an adult to thank this caring teacher for his devotion and what he had done for me. He contributed so much to my professional life. I had the good fortune—with the help of the Internet—to find and meet his son and grandson more than sixty years later on February 2008 at the inauguration of the Mémorial of the Internment and Deportation of Royallieu in Compiègne.

After graduating from high school, I did not know what to do. I was offered opportunities to take over some small businesses and to continue the tradition of my parents by being a merchant. When it came to education, I had no model or guidance in the family or among friends of the family. Around me, almost everyone got a job at an early age, around fourteen or fifteen years old, without any skills. They learned on the job. That was the way it was then. No one in the family was able to help me with this critical decision. No one in the family had gone beyond the "Certificat d'Etudes Primaires," which was usually earned at the age of fourteen, except for Cécile, René's wife, who had gone on another three years to the Brevet, and Marcel, who had studied accounting for a couple of years. I really wanted to enter the University. However, if I did, I would not be able to contribute to the family income. I did not want to abuse the generosity of Papa Henri and Maman Suzanne.

Finally I decided to go and study mechanical engineering in a vocational school. I took up drafting, mechanical design, and working with machine tools. After graduation, I was hired by a government agency called the "Ponts et Chaussées" (Bridges and Roads). The work consisted of doing land surveys to eventually build roads, bridges, water and sewer lines for new housing developments. The work itself was interesting but with a limited future. In addition, two office workers in their fifties to whom I reported to, gave me, the youngest recruit, the very embarrassing daily assignment of getting them bottles of cheap red wine. I had to go and buy it at a grocery store across the street from our office. They kept the bottles in their desk drawers within easy reach. I hated this disgraceful task that was forced on me. It was degrading. I hid the bottles as best as I could under my jacket when coming back from the grocery store to the office. I was petrified of the possibility of an encounter with the Director of the agency in the staircase that was the only way to the office. What could I have told him? That it was not for me? I would have had to tell him the truth, and that would probably have cost me my job. Those two long-term employees were more important to him than I was. Fortunately, I was never caught performing this degrading task. I volunteered for fieldwork to stay away from the office as often as possible

The working conditions were not very motivating. After about a year, I decided to look for a new opportunity. I was offered a position as a mechanical designer with a manufacturer of sophisticated equipment specializing in complex high-speed machinery to produce glass bottles. Work was very interesting and I was able to fully use my education. There were about fifteen designers in the office. The discipline was strict. We were not allowed to speak to each other unless it was for work. If a conversation lasted more than a few minutes the chief engineer would come to our working space and ask if we needed help. Although, I liked the work, I could not see myself spending my whole life there. It was too restrictive. One of my colleagues in the design group close to retirement strongly recommended that I think of a more stimulating career.

I was only eighteen years old, the youngest in the engineering group. For some ambiguous reason, I did not want to show too much ambition for fear of alienating others, particularly people who had been in this group ten to twenty years at about the same level as I was. Again, I wanted to hide my jewishness.

The way out was to further my education. I enrolled in the University of Paris to study Mechanical Engineering. For two years until I graduated I took the forty-five minute train ride twice a week to Paris on Wednesdays after work from six o'clock to midnight and on Saturdays all day.

I graduated in 1959. The same year I was called for military duty in the French Air Force. France had been at war in Algeria since 1954. Because I was a war orphan, I was exempt from service on the front line in Algeria. I served on a number of Air Force bases. The first one was Compiègne, the same place used by the Germans as an Internment and Deportation camp. By a strange coincidence, forty-eight years later, in February 2008, I stood in the same room where I slept for the first six months of my military service and gave a speech about World War II and the courageous acts of the Ribouleau family on the occasion of the inauguration of the Memorial of the Internment and Deportation.

Transitioning from civilian to military life was extremely difficult. One loses his freedom, physically and mentally. For the first three months we slept in large dorms. The distance between the beds was sufficient for a person to move sideways. All the recruits came from different backgrounds, wealthy, middle class, and less fortunate. Most of us were in our early twenties. One of us, at twenty-six, was considered old. He had deferred the mandatory age to complete a priesthood education. We had to conform to the same dress code, a pair of blue dungarees every day, all day. We had to get used to obeying orders, to get up, to wash, to eat and to go to bed at fixed times.

At 9 p.m. when the lights went out, interesting conversations took place. The darkness freed people from their inhibitions. It helped some in talking and confessing their misdeeds and deep-buried thoughts. A Parisian roughneck recounted, as he was half crying, that he had raped a young girl in a Paris suburb. He would never have confessed such a crime in daylight. He asked us how to get away from the gang life. Another one, son of wealthy parents, promised to help him with contacts. I doubt they ever saw or talked to each other again after we had completed our training. That rich kid often got parcels with champagne, caviar, exotic breads, chocolates, and other expensive goodies that he would share with some of us. Our conversations in the dark often turned to sex! The rich fellow told us that a number of married women, friends of his parents and much older than him would invite him to luxurious hotels in Paris. He was convinced that making love with socks on was very erotic! The fellow who had studied to be a priest told us that even if he decided not to become a priest, he would remain a virgin until he got married. These confessions, exchanges of ideas and comparisons of social behaviors opened our minds. During these few months we were all equal, almost.

I listened and spoke little. I never shared my childhood. I did hide as best as I could my Jewish origins. I was still in denial.

I spent six months in a military school in eastern France where I learned electronic communication. After completing the course, I was sent to the Air Force bases of Tours and Orleans, south of Paris. I was bored. I was thinking of all the interesting things I could be doing in civilian life. The war in Algeria was not going anywhere. More and more soldiers were getting killed. There were now many attacks on soldiers on the French mainland. Although we were not authorized to wear civilian clothes even while on leaves, we quickly took our uniform off as soon as we left the base.

The mandatory 18-month duty was extended month to month. After twenty-eight long months, I was released at last.

I went back to my former employer in Compiègne.

Before serving in the Armed Forces, I had met my future wife, Sylviane, at a cousin's wedding. She worked as a seamstress at a clothing store in her hometown, Blois, south of Paris. We were married in March 1960. Our son, Olivier was born September 15, 1962. I saw my son coming into our world, and at that moment I thought of the happiness my parents would have felt if they could have been with us at the birth of their first grandson. I could see us embracing each other sharing this wonderful moment. With the birth of Olivier, the Malmed name would survive.

A few months after the birth of Olivier I accepted an engineering position with a large tire manufacturer located in Clermont-Ferrand, an industrial city halfway between Paris and the Méditerranéan Sea. In Clermont-Ferrand, we lived in a comfortable apartment provided by my employer. I was assigned to a trainee area. There were many factories in the town, all belonging to our company. From the outside, most of them resembled a jail rather than a manufacturing and office facility. Large iron doors opened up at 7:45 a.m. to let the employees come in and closed at 8 a.m.

They reopened at 12 p.m. to let everyone out for lunch. The routine was repeated at 1:30 p.m. and in the evening. All the departments were very specialized and isolated from each other.

After a few months, I heard that the company was expanding to the United States. I was very interested. I inquired and was told that I should be patient and that it might take a few years before there would be openings for people with my background.

My sister and I continued to write to each other every other week. Home phones were still rare. I learned about her wedding, the birth of her daughters, her fight against tuberculosis. The disease was discovered when her first daughter Anita was eighteen months old and resulted in a ten-month stay at the Rockefeller Institute Hospital in New York. In 1953, there was little treatment for tuberculosis except isolation and complete bed rest. She survived. We exchanged pictures. We were able to maintain a precious relationship during the many years we were separated.

In 1963, fourteen years after our separation, Rachel came back to France for a visit with her husband Izzy. At the time, we lived in Clermont-Ferrand, about three hundred miles south of Paris. Rachel and Izzy were scheduled to land in Paris at Orly airport in the early morning. When we arrived at the airport, impatient to welcome them we learned that the baggage handlers were on strike and that the plane would be diverted to Brussels, Belgium, several hundred miles north of Paris. Compiègne happens to be located between Brussels and Paris. We were told that the passengers would be brought back to Paris by bus.

We drove to Compiègne hoping that we would have more information as to where we should go next. Rachel, upon landing in Brussels, had called and spoken to Papa Henri. When we arrived in Compiègne, Papa Henri and Marcel were on their way to meet the bus. It would take several hours before they arrived. It was a beautiful day. We brought out chairs on the sidewalk, sat down and waited.

I checked my watch constantly thinking, *"Let's hope they don't get a flat tire. Let's hope they don't have mechanical problems. Let's hope that they don't have an accident."*

After a long time, I was so nervous that I could no longer sit there. I went inside the house and started to shave, which in the rush and being so concerned about being late, I had not done in the morning. I had one side shaved when I heard, "They are here! They are here!"

I quickly wiped the shaving cream off my face and rushed outside. Marcel's car, a Renault "Fregate" was pulling in front of the house. The doors opened. I saw a very beautiful young woman, elegantly dressed in a blue suit with white gloves. We looked at each other for a few seconds and found ourselves in each other's arms. Fourteen years had gone by since we had last seen each other or heard each other's voices.

We were all in tears. I did not want to let go of Rachel. Emotions were strong. At last, I spoke her name and was able to say, "Rachel, is it really you? I am not dreaming?"

"No, you are not dreaming. I am here. I am back." She said between sobs.

A tall young man was standing next to her, smiling. I recognized Izzy, my sister's husband, from the pictures Rachel had sent me. He kissed me awkwardly. I learned later on that men rarely kiss each other in America. He said something in English. I did not understand. I was so shocked that I could not think of any English words. Rachel became the translator.

The three weeks they were with us went by fast. We had so much to catch up, so many memories to revisit, so many people to see and so many places to go. We talked about the arrest of our parents, the difficulties during wartime, our stay in Saint-Quentin, Rachel's departure to the United States. We went to see the house where we lived with our parents and with Papa Henri and Maman Suzanne.

New owners occupied the first-floor apartment. They welcomed us warmly and let us visit the two empty apartments we had lived in from 1940 to 1946. We went down to the basement and the cellar where we had spent so many days and nights. The bomb shelter Papa Henri had built by the chicken coop was no longer there. The mound of dirt against the back wall of the garden, where I climbed to escape the SS on their last attempt to arrest us, was still there. In that pile Marcel had buried a machine gun that he had taken from a downed allied airplane in the adjacent field. The block that had been used to decapitate the duck that had flown away headless was still in the courtyard. So many memories! The only recollection I had of our parents was the day of their arrest. Rachel talked of their kindness and love for us. We spoke of the Ribouleau family, of their immense courage, of their kindness and love for us.

Izzy was eager to see Paris. He knew of the French capital from American TV and magazines. He told us, without having seen it, that he thought it was the most beautiful city in the world!

Salomon, our cousin who lived in the center of France joined us in Paris. We shared again memories of our stay in Saint-Quentin. We recalled our chaotic lives during and after the war. We felt a strong urge to talk about this period.

The day went by fast. All of us, Rachel, Izzy, Salomon, Sylviane, my wife, and I did a lot in one day. We saw the Eiffel Tower, Notre-Dame, the Sacré-Coeur, and the Memorial of the Unknown Jew. We took a boat ride on the Seine river and walked the Champs Elysées. At the end of the day, it was difficult to leave Salomon. We went to Saint-Quentin to visit with Uncle and Aunt Blum. I had not seen them since I left Saint-Quentin, twelve years ago. It was a tense reunion. Rachel was happy and proud to introduce Izzy to them.

I was still angry with them, but I did my best to be cordial and to hide my still-strong resentment. I did not want to spoil the day. I hoped that it would help me forget the painful memories of our separation from the Ribouleau family, from my sister, and of my unhappy four-year stay with them. We went to Blois, and visited with my wife's parents and saw many of the Loire Valley castles. Rachel and Izzy loved every minute of it. Everything was so different for them, even for Rachel who had never been south of Paris. She lived a very happy life in the United States. She was still hopeful that I would join her there.

Izzy adored France. He had never been outside of the United States prior to this trip. The modest means of his family never allowed him to travel. His curious nature made him ask many questions. I learned much about my brother-in-law in the month we spent together. He was an inventor. Without a college degree, he enjoyed a brilliant career as an entrepreneur. He shared with me new products ideas he was working on. It was exciting and of great interest to me. Our backgrounds were complementary. He was very persistent in trying to persuade me to immigrate to the United States, pointing out that my sister had been dreaming for years for us to be reunited. He was certain that we could have a much better life than we could ever hope for in France.

He was so right!

My professional prospects in France were limited. I listened very attentively to his arguments. I was also thinking of all the difficulties that I would need to overcome if we decided to emigrate, such as convincing my wife who did not speak a word of English and who was close to her family, leaving behind Papa Henri and Maman Suzanne, leaving a secure job, selling our furniture and our car, moving to a country we had never been to, etc.

Saying goodbye to my sister and brother-in-law was very difficult. This time we knew we would not have to wait fourteen years before we would see each other again.

After their departure, Sylviane and I talked about this "crazy" thought of moving to America. Was it an opportunity?

The tense atmosphere, the stifling working conditions, and the presence of this anti-Semitic coworker in Clermont-Ferrand, who constantly taunted me with his insults, weighed in my decision. I also realized that it would be difficult to move ahead in the French industry without the help of influential people, which I did not have access to. I could not see myself spending my whole life waiting for a doubtful promotion, a yearly salary increase, the next vacation and retirement. I was struck by the apathy of most employees, the lack of excitement for their job. I was also surprised by the gap between management and employees. I needed to be surrounded with people who shared my passion for the company and its products. I needed to broaden my knowledge, my horizons, to feel that I was contributing to the growth of the organization. I also longed to be close to my sister.

The thought of emigrating became increasingly attractive. We knew it would not be easy but we could not let this opportunity pass by. The grey, comfortable, life ahead of us in France lacked the challenge I was looking for. Sylviane was pregnant with our second child. Leaving France meant leaving a nice apartment, new furniture, a fairly new car, good friends, a beautiful region of France and our families for the "unknown."

After many days of heart wrenching deliberations we decided to accept Izzy and Rachel's offer to immigrate to the United States. We were excited by the prospect of a new life in a new world.

I was 27, Sylviane, 25 and Olivier a year old.

# Chapter 22

# Another parting

February 1964, we boarded the magnificent ocean liner, SS France, in the harbor of "Le Havre" on the coast of French Brittany. The amount of luggage as well as the high price of air fare made us decide to choose the sea route. The prospect of spending five days on this luxury ship at sea was also quite attractive. The SS France with its 1035 ft length and its two thousand passengers capacity was one of the largest steamers of its day. This was its second voyage. We had no inkling of what the Atlantic crossing was going to be.

During the boarding process, the atmosphere was chaotic with people and luggage everywhere. There were many immigrants among the passengers. Families did not want to let go of each other. When would they see each other again? For many, it would be never. There was a lot of hugging, kissing and tearful faces. We held our son Olivier's hand tight for fear of losing him in the unruly crowd. He was eighteen months old. Daniel Monier, our brother-in-law, the husband of my wife's sister had accompanied us to take delivery of our car, a Renault R4, which he had bought from us.

A few days before our departure we visited with Papa Henri and Maman Suzanne. Saying goodbye was very painful. I was overwhelmed with guilt about leaving them. They were very troubled with our decision to immigrate, probably thinking that we would never see each other again. They understood my desire to improve our conditions and my longing to be close to my sister. However, it was extremely difficult for them to accept that I would be moving so far away. A year and a half earlier, I remember the dismayed look when I told them that I had accepted a new position and we had to move to Clermont-Ferrand, an eight-hour car ride from Compiègne in those days.

Now, I was telling them we were moving to another continent across the Atlantic Ocean. They could not comprehend that I would leave such a secure job with a large and successful company they considered to be one of the best. In France it was customory to stay with the same company until retirement. Changing employers frequently was frowned upon and would make you seem unstable. My decision surprised and even shocked them. I can still see the concerned look when I broke the news. Papa Henri said in a sad voice, "Son, I hope you have thought this decision out carefully. I hope that you are not making a mistake."

He had kissed Olivier and said: "Let's hope that you get used to an entirely new life."

Maman Suzanne was crying as she hugged us. It was a very emotional separation.

I was thinking of my parents, forever young in my mind. Would I be able to move away from them if they were alive? Would they approve of this departure? They probably would have been happy to know that Rachel and I would be reunited. If our parents were alive, it is improbable that Rachel would have immigrated to the United States in the first place.

It was so difficult to leave behind the people who were so dear to me, with whom we shared so many painful and so many good memories: the family dinners, the holiday get-togethers, the family card games, the fishing trips, and the bad ones as well—the French police taking our parents away, shattering my childhood, the ever-present fear. I felt that by leaving France I was closing the door on a past that I had been trying so hard to forget.

*The question was, could I ever forget? A new life was waiting. What will it be?*

The personnel aboard the SS France made us feel like royalty. We were not used to such luxury. There was a swimming pool, a movie theater, several bars, reading lounges, and a nursery for the children. We would have liked to take advantage of all of it but the weather decided otherwise for us. The crossing of the Atlantic did not turn out as we had fantasized. Our cabin located at the rear of the boat on top of the mechanical stabilizers was extremely noisy. We met a terrible storm the first night crossing the channel from Le Havre to London. The sea was unleashed. And it did not get much better from London to New York. The waves seemed to be as high as the ship. Despite the enormous size of the boat, it felt like we were a cork in this immense ocean. Sylviane, my wife, who was pregnant, was terribly seasick.

In the morning, we managed to walk from our cabin to the nursery to drop off Olivier and then find a lounge chair in the middle of the boat, with the least motion. The pitching was such that we had to use the railing to move around. When the seas calmed down for a few hours we went to the magnificent dining room. The plates and utensils were attached to the tables so that they would not fly off. Altogether we missed quite a number of delicious meals.

Our son, Olivier was the only one in our family who did not suffer from sea sickness. Fortunately we were able to leave him at the day-care center all day. It would have been very difficult for us to take care of him.

Given the sea conditions, the conversations with other passengers were held to a minimum. As much as we would have liked to take advantage of the amenities of this luxurious boat, we couldn't wait to be on land again.

It was our first trip to the United States. What we knew of the country where we planned to spend the rest of our lives was from American movies, many cowboy movies, limited TV coverage, news reports, photos Rachel had sent us, and from books we had read. About a year prior to our decision to move to the United States, an American couple, friends of my sister and brother-in-law, had visited with us and had told us about the good life in America. We had very little knowledge of what was awaiting at the end of the journey. It simply was not possible to anticipate what America was going to be like for us.

At last the five-day crossing that felt a lot longer than five days was ending as our ship entered the New York Harbor at 5:00 a.m. on February 22, 1964. All passengers on the different bridges were looking at the New York skyline. The sight we were all so anxiously looking to see was the Statue of Liberty. We could see it in the far distance. It represented for us America and "Freedom." It is difficult to describe the feelings I had as we passed by this beautiful landmark. Pictures do not pay justice to its beauty and splendor and what it represents for an immigrant. At that moment, seeing the Statue of Liberty I thought I knew why I had decided to immigrate to the USA. Subconsciously I was looking for anything that would confirm that

I had made the right decision. Uprooting my family from a comfortable life was scary. Freedom meant to me a lot more than physical freedom. In France I felt prisoner of my Jewish identity. I could
never justify nor forget the collaboration of the French police and the
French administration with the Nazis. It was too often on my mind.
The Jew-hater I had worked with for close to a year was a constant re-
minder that there were many more like him.

Twenty years after the war ended, these people were still
around. I knew what I was leaving behind, although I did not know
what was ahead. I had so much hope, so many expectations. I may
even have been looking for the American soldiers who had liberated us, those cool soldiers chewing gum, gliding with their silent
boots over the cobble stones of Compiègne at dawn on September
first, 1944! The sounds and the image of a pair of boots passing by
our cellar window that night are still very much present.

The SS France passed under the gigantic Verrazano Nar-
rows Bridge that connects Brooklyn to Staten Island, then under
construction.

We had been up since 4 a.m. At about 8 a.m. we finally docked.
The passengers were impatient to disembark. It took several hours
to go through immigration and customs. Free and on firm ground at
last, we rushed into Rachel and Izzy's arms. Close to a year had gone
by since we saw each other in France. We filled their station wagon
with all our luggage. Besides our clothes, Olivier's toys, photo al-
bums, silver tableware that belonged to our parents that Papa Henri
and Maman Suzanne had kept preciously for their return, we had
also brought a Moped called "Mobylette" in French for Izzy.

New York was very cold in February. The sky was a pure blue. It
had snowed the day before and the snow was everywhere and dirty.
The sidewalks were full of pedestrians. They all seemed in a hurry,
like in most large cities, and probably eager to get out of the cold.
Many yellow taxis were beeping their horns impatiently. My first
impression of the US was not what I thought it would be. I was no
longer sure of what I was expecting. Once we left New York City we
discovered streets lined with trees and pretty houses set back from
the street by lawns covered with snow. We were surprised to see no
walls or fences separating the street from the houses.

My sister lived in a small town called New Hyde Park on Long
Island, about twenty five miles from New York City. Our nieces,

Anita twelve years old, and Helene, eight, were waiting impatiently at home for our arrival. They had heard so much about us for such a long time.

It was planned for us to stay with Rachel and Izzy until we found an apartment. Anita had accepted to let us have her room, a decision she quickly regretted, as sleeping in the basement was not a good trade. Both our nieces were looking curiously at the three immigrants as though we were from another world. Most of their attention was devoted toward their cousin Olivier, who looked like a doll in his pale blue coat and matching hat. Sylviane was eager to lie down and rest after this trying trip. She was not able to communicate and felt isolated. She was already missing her family and friends. The neighbors and family who had heard of us for many years and especially in the last twelve months were curious and happy to meet us. I was self-conscious of my English and was concerned about making myself look like a fool. I found it quite difficult to understand American English. All my English teachers in France had a British accent. Thankfully, my sister was there and helped answer the questions people were asking us. We were tired and disoriented.

A few days after our arrival we visited with Aunt Rose, who had welcomed Rachel into her home in the United States fifteen years prior. We met our cousin Eileen, her husband Irwin, and our cousin Irving. We were discovering a new side of our family we only read about in Rachel's letters. Everywhere we went, we were treated like VIP's. People were very nice and encouraging, understanding our doubts and disarray, I guessed. Some of them were immigrants themselves and had experienced the feelings of doubt we had. We were quite impressed by the size of the houses and puzzled by the beautiful furniture covered with transparent plastic that made it quite uncomfortable to sit on.

My first American experience happened shortly after our arrival. A friend of Izzy's invited us to his home. He took us to his garage where his shiny and enormous Cadillac was parked. To my surprise and excitement he invited me to drive it. I was thrilled. I promised myself right then and there that someday I would own a Cadillac. I did keep this promise in 2013!

A few days after our arrival, I started to work for my brother-in-law Izzy, who was the director of a research and development laboratory for a lawn mower manufacturer. I was impressed that

Izzy would entrust me with so many reponsiblities almost immediately. I was not used to being asked to test myself beyond my
known abilities. I was involved in all phases of engineering and
manufacturing. I learned more in the first year working with my
brother-in-law than I had learned since I started to work in France
at the age of 17.

We quickly moved to an apartment in Queens close to work
and to my sister's home, happy and nervous to be on our own. Both
Sylviane and I felt handicapped by the language barrier. Everything was so different and foreign to us. We missed our friends, our
French routines and our Sunday escapes in the mountains. The rent
for this apartment was about four times what we were paying in Clermont-Ferrand and a lot less comfortable. It was old and dark. We
acquired used furniture.

Once a month, the large objects to be trashed were collected
by the city sanitation department. My sister's neighbors across the
street had put out on the sidewalk a mattress that appeared to me
almost new. I quickly picked it up and stored it in my sister's garage.
After I heard Rachel name all the sicknesses we could contract by
sleeping on this mattress, I quickly, put it back on the curb!

Soon after moving in, we discovered that our kitchen was infested with cockroaches. We had never seen such pests. They were
so fast it was easy to think that we could be hallucinating. They
would hide in the pantry and in the drawers. We would see them
mostly at night. When we turned the lights on they disappeared
faster than our brain could register. A service company came and
fumigated the apartment. We were rid of these beasts for a while
until our neighbor below us did the same. We were infested again.

By the time we paid for our trip to the U.S., we had less than
$1,000 in our pocket. After buying a used car and having paid two
months rent deposit we were out of money. Thankfully, I did get a
paycheck weekly.

Sylviane was six months pregnant and spent most of the days in
the apartment alone with Olivier. Without language skills it was difficult for her to communicate and make friends. The visits with her
gynecologist were difficult due to her limited English. We started to
wonder if our decision to immigrate had been a good one.

After a very long and difficult childbirth Sylviane delivered a
baby girl. She died forty-eight hours later. The American dream was

turning into an American nightmare. We had been looking forward so much to our American baby girl.

We were overwhelmed with grief. There were so many difficulties to absorb, this unexpected death of our baby, the foreign language barrier and all new ways of life. What should have been a happy event had turned into a tragedy.

Why? Maybe we did not understand the doctor's instructions, maybe this would not have happened in France, maybe Sylviane's unhappiness during the last few months of pregnancy had contributed to this catastrophe? Many questions without answers nagged me.

My work kept me busy and satisfied. I traveled often to the factory located near Cincinnati. There I helped with setting up the manufacturing of the products we had designed in New York. I was making good progress in learning the language and the American ways to communicate, quite different from the French ones.

It was extremely difficult to overcome the sadness of losing our daughter. Going back to France was still in our thoughts, but we did not have the required funds. After fifteen years of separation from my sister, I could not see us being separated again. Our used car was constantly breaking down. I spent many weekends repairing it. During one of these repair sessions, the car caught on fire, caused by electric wires touching each other. Izzy, my brother-in-law who was helping me, saved the car by disconnecting the burning wire with his bare hands. On the social front, we missed our family and friends, and we were wondering if we could ever get used to the ways of living in this country. Would we be able to cross what seemed then to be an enormous gap?

In the evenings, we watched TV. It took us several months before we could start to understand enough to make sense of what we were seeing and hearing. The English I had learned in school in France was quite different from the American English, accent, expressions, and mostly speed of speech.

I still felt guilty about abandoning Papa Henri and Maman Suzanne. Their unhappiness with our leaving France was unsettling. As soon as we arrived in the States, I wrote them a number of letters. No answer. I continued to write every week. It was very troubling. It took several months before I received Papa Henri's first letter. It was a heartwarming letter responding to my comments and giving us news of the family. I read it several times. A heavy weight was lifted from my chest. We continued to write each other about once a month for the next twenty years until he passed away.

Our first year in America, I was constantly hungry and I ate much, maybe due to anxiety. Izzy predicted that I soon would not be able to fit through the door of the office. Fortunately, his prediction did not materialize. Shortly after we had moved to our apartment, as we were walking in the neighborhood we passed by a bakery with enticing cakes displayed in the window. We could not resist and bought one. We were impatient to finish lunch to taste this appetizing cake. The cake was so sweet that after a few bites we gave up! We were not used to so much sugar in food. So much for American pastry!

At work I greatly appreciated the differences of doing business. It was so good to feel free to suggest, to argue, to take initiatives without the fear of making mistakes. I was becoming increasingly confident in myself. In the French companies I had been associated with, there was always a distrustful, stifling environment and a feeling of being under constant surveillance. I was enjoying the newly acquired freedom and confidence in my capabilities.

A year went by fast. Despite the doubts, the difficulties of adapting, we were starting to love this new country.

We knew, then, that America was our home.

# Chapter 23

# The American Dream

As time went on, we adjusted to our new life. Learning to speak English correctly remained a challenge. We were able, with some difficulty, to follow TV shows. I wished we had the capability then to rewind so that we could listen a second or third time. When I was able to understand most of the evening news, I felt I had made a breakthrough. Sylviane was struggling but was making progress. The ability to communicate gave us the opportunity to make new friends. It was a relief to see my wife coming out of her isolation.

A year to the day after the birth and death of our first baby girl, Corinne was born on May 6, 1965. This time, fortunately, the delivery went smoothly. Corinne was a beautiful and healthy baby. We were proud and happy parents. We had hoped to have a baby girl and we felt very lucky to have our wish fulfilled.

"She has your eyes, Leon!" said Rachel excitingly.

"She is the spitting image of her mother," countered Izzy.

Those were moments of great happiness. We all felt very close to each other.

Once again, our parents would have been so happy to be here with us for the birth of their granddaughter. I am sure they would have loved to hold her in their arms, sing lullabies, probably in Yiddish, as my mother had done for me when I was a baby. The Nazis had deprived her and my father of the great and simple joy of becoming grandparents.

A year after immigrating we still lived in the same apartment in Floral Park, Queens, a borough of New York City. We had a new dream—owning our own home. For the next year we lived on a very strict budget to save for the down payment of our future home. We did not go out much. We spent most of our weekends on the beautiful beaches of Long Island in the summer. When the weather prevented us from going out, we would play with Olivier's

*Corinne, Sylviane, Leon, Olivier New York 1967*

and Corinne's paint-by-number games. After many hours of patient work we ended up with a masterpiece!

To boost our income I gave French lessons to American families planning to travel to France or simply wanting to learn French.

Some new friends who had immigrated from France invited us to their home. They lived in Hicksville, Long Island, about thirty miles east of New York City. We liked the area and started to look for a home. After a few months of house hunting we found one within our budget. In the summer of 1966 we moved into our new home in Hicksville.

To avoid mowing the lawn, the former owners, who were the artist type, had attempted to replace the grass with white stones. Unfortunately it did not prevent the weeds from growing between the stones. We spent many weekends picking up the small stones one by one. After lots of backbreaking work, we finally had a beautiful lawn.

It felt wonderful to live in our own home. We were proud. We had succeeded in fulfilling our dream. We were a happy couple with two beautiful children, a boy and a girl. We had a new car, a Ford Coupe. We were healthy. What more would we want?

Nothing lasts forever, as I would soon learn. Surprises and rocky times lay ahead.

Rachel and I invited Papa and Maman Ribouleau to come and visit with us. To our great joy, they accepted. We quickly sent them airline tickets, concerned that if we did not do it immediately they might change their mind. In 1975, eleven years after we immigrated, we welcomed them at New York's JFK airport. They spent two weeks with us. Two great weeks. We took them to New York City, to the beaches of Long Island, and to shopping centers. Shopping malls were not popular in France at the time, certainly not in Compiègne.

We introduced them to our family and friends. Rachel took them to the Synagogue she and Izzy belonged to for the Saturday Service. They were presented to the local Jewish community. Everyone was quite surprised when the cantor intoned a religious melody on the French national hymn "La Marseillaise." Papa Henri and Maman Suzanne became emotional. They stood up. Papa Henri kept his right hand on his heart for the duration of the song. The whole Congregation was so moved that, contrary to custom, they stood up and applauded. More than thirty years later some of the people who were there on that day still talk about this very special moment.

The two weeks went by fast. I took Papa Henri fishing while Sylviane took Maman Suzanne shopping. As Papa and I sat side by side waiting for the fish to bite we reminisced about the times we used to sit on the banks of the river Oise in Compiègne. We talked about the large motorized barges we cursed when they came too close to shore at high speed and would disturb our fishing. Despite these small annoyances they were happy times on another continent three thousand seven hundred miles away.

We were together again for a short and precious two weeks.

With the children in school, Sylviane, who by now spoke fairly good English, began to look for a job. She found a position with Air France as a ground hostess. She asked her sister to come from France and live with us to help with the children. Martine accepted and soon moved in with us. After a few months, wanting to broaden her horizons, she took a job in a French restaurant in New York City.

Since Sylviane was an airline employee, our family benefited from very low international airfares. We took advantage of the op-

*Rachel, Maman Suzanne, Leon, Papa Henri, New York 1975*

portunity to travel. A number of times we flew from New York to France for a long weekend and spent two or three days with Papa and Maman Ribouleau. They always welcomed us with open arms. They spent all the summers at their second home in a tiny village called "Le Viviers," on the banks of the Loire river about a hundred miles south of Paris, and a few miles from Blois, Sylviane's hometown. Papa Henri was also born in this region.

Olivier and Corinne spent their summer vacations in France almost every summer. They loved to be with Papa Henri and Maman Suzanne. They quickly learned French. At home in the U.S. they were reluctant to speak French with us although they were fluent. They did not want to be different from their peers.

After working with Izzy for a couple of years, I accepted a new position as a development engineer. Shortly thereafter I was promoted to Manufacturing Manager, with one hundred and fifty employees reporting to me. I was proud of having been entrusted with such an important job. My intimate knowledge of the products I had designed prior to the promotion and the manufacturing technology I had learned with Izzy helped me a great deal. I worked six days a week and came home late most days. I loved my job.

Two years later, I was offered the opportunity to start a company to develop and manufacture high-technology products. A French investor who was looking to expand into the American market financed this start-up. That was a dream job with great potential.

Here again, I continued to spend many hours at work. When I came home late in the evening, which was often, Olivier and Corinne were asleep. I would open their bedroom door and kiss them gently so they would not wake up.

A modest immigrant from a small French town who could have spent his life vegetating in a company in France was now Executive Vice President and General Manager of a high-tech American company. Was I dreaming?

I was so proud. I was convinced that this hard work made my family happy as well. I was blind. I did not realize the widening of a gap between my wife and I. If I perceived it, I ignored it.

One evening in 1976 Sylviane told me, abruptly, that she wanted a separation. Seconds, maybe minutes went by before I registered what I was being told. Finally the blood came back to my brain and

I understood what she was saying, I was stunned. My legs would not support me.

"Wh—, wh—, wh—, what are you saying?" I asked, stammering. I was looking at her, totally dazed. She had gotten up and was walking back and forth nervously.

"I want us to divorce," she said forcefully.

"Divorcing? But ... why?" I said in a stupor.

I was appalled. I was crushed. The sky was falling. I loved my wife. I adored my children. I could not conceive being separated from the three of them. Everything was collapsing around me.

"I do not love you anymore. It is over between us," she said.

We had been married fifteen years.

The walls were spinning. I was devastated. I was torn apart. A cataclysm had hit me. I should have seen it coming. I remembered that my wife's attitude had changed. But I did not believe that anything like that would ever happen and certainly not so abruptly.

No, it was a nightmare. It was not real, I told myself. I would wake up.

My parents had disappeared from one day to the next. I had been forcefully separated from my second parents. My sister had been taken away from me when I was still a child. How could I survive this new tragedy? How could I remain sane, faced with this new dreadful ordeal?

My wife and my children were part of me.

Fate was against me, separating me from all the ones I loved.

"Please let us try, for our children's sake," I asked desperately.

"It is too late," Sylviane replied.

"Please," I implored.

I insisted that we see a marriage counselor. We did. The psychiatrist we chose was about sixty years old and specialized in marital problems. He was a heavy pipe smoker. I guessed listening to other people's problems all day took a toll on him, and pipe smoking provided him with some mental relief. We saw him, sometimes alone, other times together. He was very interested in my life story. I shared with him my phobia of separations. I never realized how much I feared separations until I talked to this doctor. I wanted to save our marriage. I was ready to quit my job, do anything that was required to avoid this catastrophe. After a few months of therapy, we had made good progress.

To our deep sadness, our psychiatrist died suddenly. We stopped the sessions thinking that we did not need more therapy, and we did not feel like starting with a new doctor.

Less than a year later Sylviane asked again for a separation.

"Leon, I do not feel any love for you anymore. I realize I am making you miserable. You do not deserve it. You are young enough to start a new life. It is better for both of us to separate." She said.

I knew that it meant a permanent separation.

I was desperate. I felt deep inside that I could not escape the outcome this time.

In my professional life I was able to resolve complex problems, technical, personnel, and business issues. In my personal life I could not find a solution to the most important issue. Sleepless nights succeeded each other. The anguish that I tried to hide from colleagues at work and friends was choking me.

How will I have the strength to tell my children that we will not be living together?

Eventually, I took Olivier to the local ice-cream parlor where the four of us used to go on summer nights. I explained to him, clumsily, stammering, that his mother and I would be separating. I could not think of what to say to lighten his pain, the disappointment that he would feel, if not immediately, later on. Words were failing me. I could hardly breathe. I was trying—too hard, perhaps—to find simple and reassuring words for him. The same day I did the same with Corinne. It was a day of mental torture that I remember well.

Probably shocked and scared by this unexpected and terrible news, neither of them asked questions. I had told them that I would try to live close by, and we would spend the weekends together as Sylviane and I had agreed. I felt their pain, their grief and their fear of the tomorrow on their face and in their silence. Perhaps they would even feel guilty. I promised that I will always love them and I would always be there for them.

I was in my late thirties.

I spent weekends and evenings looking for an apartment close by. I did not want to move. It was, emotionally, a very difficult task.

Why did I have to leave my house?

I could not stop searching the reasons for such an ending to fifteen years of marriage, a marriage that I thought was perfect. I did not want to live apart from my children. They were what I loved

*Olivier and Corinne, New York 1975*

most in my life. They will suffer dearly from my leaving home. These thoughts haunted me day and night. But I was given no choice. I had to go on.

Finally I moved to a furnished apartment, the first floor of a two story home. The owners, a very nice couple in their fifties, lived on the second floor. The house was one block away from the seashore which I thought would be wonderful to spend the summer weekends on the beach with my children.

I had never lived alone. It was an extremely difficult adjustment.

My job was so demanding that I was able to forget my personal worries during working hours. In the evenings I had to face the solitude and often despair. I felt very lonely. Many of our married friends, probably concerned about my bachelor status, kept their distance, with the exception of my friend Dr. Maurice Gunsberger and his wife Kathleen.

Eventually, I learned how to live alone. I learned to cook with the help of Maman Suzanne. She sent me recipes. I started to date. It was a new life, and I did not care for it. It was not what I had imagined my life would be at this age. I missed home terribly. I missed coming home and being welcomed by my wife and my children running to me. I missed helping my children with their home-work, despite the frustration it entailed at times. I missed the week-ends when we would have friends over for dinner or the four of us would go to the beach or drive to some new places.

I spent as many weekends with Olivier and Corinne as possi-ble. We would go to the movies, to the theater in New York, to the beach, skating in winter time, sailing in summer time. One Sun-day afternoon while we were sailing, a sudden unannounced squall overturned our small 18-foot sail boat. Luckily, we were close to our buoy. The harbor police rescued us.

I suffered from the loneliness. The relationships I had never lasted. I was asking myself all kinds of questions regarding my fif-teen years of marriage. Was I really ever in love with my wife? I be-lieved so. But, what did I know of love at twenty-four years old when we were married? We were so young when we first met at the wed-ding of a distant cousin. Sylviane was seventeen. I was nineteen. She was beautiful in her white bridesmaid dress. She lived in Blois. It was a long way from my hometown, Compiègne, north of Paris, but close to Papa Henri's and Maman Suzanne's summer home. We started to write to each other.

When I came back from military duty her mother, a kind per-son, insisted we should get married. Her father would never get in-volved in such discussions. I did not feel ready for marriage. I asked Sylviane for us to cool the relationship down for a while. Eventu-ally, I surrendered to the pressure of my future wife and future mother-in-law.

I had learned some hurtful lessons from this experience. I did not want to suffer the torments of another separation with a new companion and be subjected to another traumatic deception. At the same time I had reached the stage of accepting that I would never meet a woman I could trust and who could fulfill my expecta-tion. I secretly wished to find such a miraculous person.

Love is not "only" to gratify sexual needs, nor is it "only" to lead a comfortable life nor is it "only" to have a family like everyone else.

Love is something deep, sublime. It is all of that plus much more.

I had the fortune to discover it in mid-life.

Chapter 24

# Happiness, at Last

It was 1979. Sylviane and I had been divorced two years. In order to stay close to my children, I still lived in the small-furnished apartment where I had moved after our separation. I spent most weekends with Olivier and Corinne. During the week I lived alone. The women I dated confirmed it would be extremely difficult, if not impossible, to find the pearl I was looking for, the person who would become a lifelong spouse. I was getting used to my life as a single man. I found it preferable to deal with the solitude rather than engaging in a semi-satisfying long-term relationship.

Doctor Maurice Gunsberger, a pediatrician of French origin, was our children's doctor since 1966. We had become close friends. I was the best man at his second marriage. I was often invited to their home.

One evening, the phone rang—a phone call that would change the course of my life dramatically. I had no clue about what was to come.

"Leon, it's Maurice," my friend said in a cheerful voice. "Would you like to meet a wonderful person? She is a nurse in the maternity ward at the hospital where I work. She is divorced. You should meet her. If you are interested, I will get you her phone number."

"Yes ..., Maurice ... Why not?" I answered without much conviction.

Two or three days later he called me back with excitement in his voice. He told me that she was reluctant to give him her phone number. He insisted that I call her quickly before she changes her mind. After we hung up I called.

A soft voice answered. I introduced myself immediately, concerned that she would hang up before I had the opportunity to tell her about my friendship with Dr. Gunsberger. I felt or I imagined some hesitation on her part. I started to talk, not giving her a chance to find an excuse to hang up. I had no idea why I was so concerned about this person. Our telephone conversation lasted more than one hour. It was an easy two-way chat. I liked her and wanted to meet her. I built up the courage to ask her, with some fear of being turned down, if we could meet. I was waiting for her answer with anxiety. After a few seconds that seemed like minutes, she said yes.

An hour or so ago I had no idea that person existed and now, she was almost the most important person in my life...

"Is there an evening that is convenient for you?" I asked trying not to sound too anxious.

"I am busy this week," she answered.

"Yes, I understand. How about next week, like Wednesday? I can cook a French dinner for you if you wish."

"OK. Let's make it Wednesday," she said. I was amazed that she had accepted my invitation.

Our prolonged talk was so natural, so simple, so interesting. Her voice had bewitched me. I wanted to meet her badly. How does she look? How old is she? Does she have a boyfriend? She might have been polite by saying yes, not wanting to displease Dr. Gunsberger. She might call me in a few days with some excuse...

A few days after my telephone conversation with the mysterious lady, Maurice and his wife Kathleen invited me to their home to celebrate the fourth birthday of their son, Joshua. The weather was beautiful. Everyone was in the backyard by the pool. After I said hello, I went to the kitchen to get a glass of water. The doorbell rang. There was no one inside the house but me. I opened the door. A beautiful woman was standing holding the hand of a child of about three years of age. She was dressed in a white uniform, including shoes and cap. I guessed she was the governess of the child whose parents were friends of the Gunsbergers.

Literally spellbound by her beauty, I was voiceless. She was ravishing! I would have loved to switch places with the little boy so that I could feel her hand in mine. We looked at each other for what seemed like a long time without saying a word.

I heard a voice that seemed to come from afar saying:

"It's her!"

I did not understand what that meant.

"It's her," the voice repeated.

I was thinking: "Her? Who, her? Whose voice do I hear?" The voice seemed to be coming from the clouds. I was in ecstasy. I slowly came down to earth. I turned toward the voice. Ah ... Maurice was talking to me.

"It is Patricia, the nurse I told you about and whom you talked to," he said, laughing.

I looked at her. I still could not speak. She started to talk to Maurice. I understood from their conversation that the little boy's name was Jimmy and that she was not his governess but his mother.

Finally, I was back to earth. I stammered a few words at such a low voice that I was not sure I was the one speaking.

"What a surprise! I never expected to meet you today. I am so happy I did." I finally said.

"Are you still available Wednesday?"

"Yes, I am," she replied.

"Wonderful, Wednesday it is," I quickly said.

To my delight, she accepted, showing the same beautiful smile that mesmerized me a few minutes ago when I opened the door. To this day, that smile has the same effect on me.

That evening when I got home, dazzled by this beautiful woman, I started to wonder if I did not dream the whole afternoon. Until Wednesday I lived in a daze between impatience and anxiety. I dreaded any phone calls, so afraid that she would call to tell me that something had come up and she would not be able to make it.

Since my separation and subsequent divorce I had lost my self-confidence when it came to romantic relationships.

At last Wednesday evening came. I had prepared a wonderful dinner. I wanted to impress her with my French cooking. I was nervous. The clock seemed to move so slowly. Any street noise in this quiet neighborhood made me jump and raised my heart rate.

Why was I so jittery? I had never felt that way with any date before. I could not explain. Today I can. I had fallen in love at first sight, for the first time in my life. It was an unknown experience for me.

We had agreed to meet at 6 p.m.; 6:00 p.m. came and went. I watched the clock move: 6:15, 6:30, 6:45. I had the feeling that I was going to eat alone ...

At 7 p.m., I heard a car stopping in front of the house. I went and peeked through the window curtains. A beautiful young lady was coming out of her car, but she was not the woman I had met four days ago. The woman I had met was dressed in a white uniform, white stockings, white shoes, white hat, with hair pulled up under her white cap. Could it be the same person? No, it could not be. Maybe? I did not know what to think. I was perplexed. Someone was knocking at the door. I opened the door. Not knowing if it was Patricia or a person who went to the wrong address, I asked:

"Are you Patricia?"

The person I had met Saturday was beautiful. This one was gorgeous.

She was looking at me smiling like she knew me, saw my confusion and said "My sister Patricia could not come. She knew you had prepared a special dinner for her. She is terribly embarrassed and she asked me to come instead. I hope you are not disappointed." She had the same smile as her sister!

I was more than surprised. I did not know what to think. I was disappointed with myself to have, maybe, fallen in love too quickly.

I could see a strong resemblance. Maybe, they were twins? It had to be a joke. It was not.

Oh well, I was a bachelor after all.

I asked her to come in.

I was troubled. How could Patricia send her sister in her place without letting me know ahead?

"My name is Maria," the young woman said with a soft voice identical to her sister Patricia.

We had a very nice, interesting conversation during dinner. She was very surprised by the dinner I had prepared. For appetizer some delicacy, then crab stuffed shrimps, a mixed salad, several cheeses, and an apple pie with a homemade crust. She was even more impressed, she told me later, when I did the dishes, refusing her help. Maybe she had never met a man who washed the dishes on a date?

"Leon," she said, "you are such a gentleman, I need to make a confession."

She was looking at me with eyes sparkling with mischief.

"I am Patricia. When you opened the door, I could see that you did not recognize me. I thought it would be fun to make you believe you were entertaining my sister. Yes, I do have a sister named Maria. Please forgive me."

I was overwhelmed with a wave of happiness. I could hardly hold my emotions. Yes, it was love at first sight!

Patricia is a native of Colombia, South America. She came to the US with her parents in 1958 at the age of six. They first lived in Queens, a borough of New York City, the same borough we moved to when we came to the US. Her father owned a store where he sold and repaired sewing machines. Patricia was the second of ten children. She had learned very early in life to help her mother with household work and to take care of her siblings.

She was a nurse, a profession she liked very much. She worked at the maternity ward of a local hospital where Dr. Maurice Gunsberger came almost daily to see his patients. She was divorced for two years. Her son, James, was three. After this unusual first evening we saw each other almost daily. A month or so later I had to leave for five weeks on a business trip to Europe which I had scheduled months before we met. It was an important trip for my company. I was very concerned that she might be gone from my life when I came back. I did not want to leave, but I was committed to many business meetings. With the hope that she would still want to see me upon my return, I had given her my return flight information. I visited six European countries. I did not call her during the five weeks I was traveling. When I landed at JFK airport in New York and cleared Customs, she was there with her beautiful smile. I exploded with joy. She was radiant. We hugged a long time. I knew then, that, at last, I had found the happiness and the life companion I had been looking for.

It was simple, real and incredible!

I was in love. This love has endured more than thirty years.

A few months later, we decided to live together. Patricia and I moved to a newly acquired condominium within walking distance to the hospital where she worked.

After her divorce she had moved back with her parents. With eight brothers and sisters it was a full house. When she and James moved in with me, it was a difficult adjustment for James. At his grandparents' home he was the baby of the house with his aunts and uncles entertaining him. All of a sudden he was alone with us.

We decorated his bedroom with Tom and Jerry wallpaper. I built a special bed with many drawers for his toys. He had a TV in his room. I knew that it would be a difficult transition for him. I did everything possible to make him feel welcomed and loved in this new environment. I wanted him to be happy. I myself have had two fathers and two mothers. I knew it was possible to love both. James was reluctant to leave the environment he was used to, where he was happy and pampered. It took a long time before he started to show me some affection. I loved James like my own child. He was still a teenager when he asked to change his family name to mine. It made me very happy.

Eight months had passed since we first met. Despite the happiness and the comfort of our relationship, we both were enjoying, I was not thinking of marriage. I still feared another letdown. I doubted myself.

To my amazement, sometimes in February 1981, Patricia asked me, point blank "Would you like to marry me?"

I was shocked by the question. We had never talked about long-term commitment. I found it impossible to articulate anything, not knowing if I was going to laugh or cry. I did not expect such a question. I took her in my arms without saying a word and I held her tight against me for a long time with tears streaming on both our cheeks.

I was not ready to say yes and certainly I was not going to say no.

After a sleepless night, I asked Patricia in the morning:

"Were you serious yesterday? Does your marriage proposal still hold? Do you really want us to get married?"

"More than ever," she answered without hesitation. "Would you like to marry me?" she asked for the second time in the last twelve hours.

"Yes, I do. I love you," I answered very moved.

We would have liked to invite the whole world to our wedding! After many discussions and grandiose plans, we decided to have a very simple wedding. Our family and circle of friends were too large to accommodate all.

In 1981, Patricia accompanied me to a Hi-Tech convention in Las Vegas. At the outcome, we were married in the non-denominational Candle Light Chapel on the Las Vegas strip in front of two witnesses we had hired for the duration of the ceremony which lasted fifteen to twenty minutes.

That day, we drove to the Grand Canyon for a long weekend. That was our honeymoon. Patricia was driving. On the deserted road from Las Vegas to the Grand Canyon, as we were swimming in happiness and not paying attention to the speed limit, we overtook a police car, the only car we had seen in miles. The siren went on immediately. We stopped. The police officer asked us what speed we were going. Instead of answering his question since we had no idea, I said: "Sir, please, we were married less than two hours ago. It is the happiest day of our lives. Please do not give us a ticket on our wedding day."

Seeing us in our wedding clothes, a bouquet of flowers on my lap, the police officer cracked a smile and told us in a tone that he wanted to sound serious "It would be a shame if you were to hurt yourselves on such an important day."

He let us go with a warning: "Respect the speed limit!"

"Yes sir, we will!" we both responded at once. We were so relieved that he did not give us a ticket on our wedding day.

Shortly after we returned home, I shared with Patricia my early life story. I had not mustered the courage to talk about it until now. After all these years, it was still so emotional. It was bottled up tight but ready to erupt. I told her about the arrest of my parents and the eight years that followed. I described how this wonderful, courageous Ribouleau family had saved our lives, my sister's and mine. How they had given us their love and affection when we needed it so badly to overcome the painful tragedy. Patricia was listening attentively, shaken by the story.

It was the very first time in more than thirty years I was sharing my memories of the war times with anyone, except for my conversations with the psychiatrist that my first wife and I consulted to save our marriage.

"I would like to take you to France for you to meet the Ribouleau family. They are the most generous and courageous people I know. Without them I would not be here today," I told Patricia.

Soon afterwards, we went to France. Patricia had never been outside of the United States except for Colombia, her native country. Our stay in Compiègne was wonderful. She conquered the whole family with her smile, kindness, and personality. The language barrier was not a serious obstacle. She was adopted immediately. Papa Henri and Maman Suzanne congratulated me warmly for having rebuilt my life with such a beautiful and charming spouse.

"You have found a pearl, son" said Papa Henri, hugging me.

"You deserve happiness," added Maman Suzanne with a huge smile.

*Patricia and Leon's wedding in Las Vegas, 1981*

Several months after we were married, I accepted a job offer in San Jose, California. During my many business trips to the West Coast I had promised myself that one day I would live there. I loved the beauty of the West and its people. Patricia quit her job. In January 1982, we moved to Los Gatos, close to Silicon Valley. After graduating from high school in New York, my daughter Corinne came to live with us. She attended the California State University in San

Jose. My son Olivier, after graduating from the University of Buffalo, came to live with us as well.

We were happy with our three children at home. In summer we would go camping, rafting, and wind surfing. In winter, it was skiing in the Sierras. We then moved a few miles away to a house in a neighborhood where James would have friends of his own age. We soon had a menagerie: three cats, a dog named Cookie, a turtle, a white rat, a snake with white and black rings, and birds. When we traveled we had a difficult time finding people to take care of all our animals. On one occasion, we could not find someone to take care of James' white rat, so we took him to New York in Patricia's handbag. We were visiting my sister and brother-in-law. The rat stayed hidden in a closed bag during our few days stay.

My sister, who was extremely scared of rodents, has never known about this uninvited guest until she reads this book!

James traded his snake for two ducklings. One of them managed to drown in a pan filled with water within a day. Unusual fate for a duck! We named the survivor "Daphne." It grew quickly. When I got home in the evening, he would tap on the sliding door of the kitchen with his beak, reminding me to go swimming with him in the pool! He would follow me all the time. When I dove into the pool he would jump and swim next to me. Too bad he was so messy. We could not keep him around. We gave him to a friend who had a farm with a pond. There he became attached to a horse and a goat. He followed them as if they were his parents. He lived there about two years. One day, probably unable to resist the attraction of the flock, he joined a flight of wild ducks that had stopped at our friend's pond.

Patricia and I belonged to a gym and a club of roller skaters. We learned how to dance the tango and the waltz on roller skates. During one of the first lessons, as I was learning to skate backwards, I fell into a large pan that had been placed there to retrieve rain water from the leaky roof. I ended up with a wet bottom, entertaining my fellow skaters.

James was growing up. Corinne graduated from college. She worked for a medical equipment company. Olivier worked for a large Silicon valley computer company.

My work, as always, kept me very busy. I specialized in the hi-tech field of digital data storage. Two years after moving to California I was promoted to Vice President of Sales and Marketing

Worldwide, traveling a lot in the US, and to Europe and Asia. I was always concerned about leaving Patricia so many times. She never complained; she understood that it was my job. I had not forgotten the setbacks and the end of my first marriage.

Patricia kept busy with a charity group helping poor school children. At a fund raising event for this organization she won the door prize, a one week rental of a home in Tahoe, a few blocks away from the lake. She went with James early in the week. I joined her on the weekend. We loved the area, the smell of the pine trees, the beautiful blue Lake Tahoe surrounded by high mountain peaks. As we were leaving town, on Easter Day we noticed a real estate office with an "Open" sign in the window.

"Let's stop for a minute. I am curious to find out what the price of a home is," I said. I had a three-day beard. I was wearing "very" used jeans. As we introduced ourselves to the agent I noticed that he was looking at me suspiciously. I guess I did not look like the ideal customer for a home on the lake.

"Excuse me sir, we are curious as to the pricing of houses near the lake," I asked.

He replied, "You see," still looking at my overused jeans, my beard, and disheveled hair, "these houses are probably not in your price range, I recommend that you look at our very affordable mobile homes."

"Oh no, we are not interested in mobile homes at this time. We want to know the price of homes on the water! Can you can show us some?" I asked.

"I am alone today. I don't have much time." the sales agent said.

He finally agreed and said, "I can only show you one."

And we loved it. The view was beautiful. From the balcony, we could see the ski area Heavenly Valley, only four or five miles away. It was very tempting.

"What do you think?" I asked Patricia.

"You are really thinking about buying a home here?" She responded.

"Why not?"

We spent many succeeding weekends in Tahoe, looking at many homes all around the Lake. After two months we decided to make an offer on the first home we had seen on Easter Day.

We went back to see our suspicious real estate agent. This time, he gave us a much warmer welcome. My better appearance probably had something to do with it. I was shaved. My hair was combed and I had clean trousers! A longtime dream to have a home on the water with a boat dock in the backyard surrounded by beauty had come true. We spent most of our weekends in Tahoe.

I often think of all the people who have helped me to be alive and to enjoy a happy life. My adult life has brought me so much after such a difficult childhood. My thoughts turn often toward my parents, and I reflect on their miserable childhood and their tragic and horrible deaths. Their suffering is often on my mind.

Corinne was married in 1993. Her son, Jake, was born in 1997. Olivier was married in 1996. His first son, Rayce, was born in 1997 and the second, Rhyder, in 2002.

The birth of our grandsons was, for Patricia and myself, a very touching event. Our anxiety in the hospital was intense. I felt great happiness when I saw my grandsons shortly after their birth. These were times when I missed my parents the most. I can imagine the joy they would have felt, had they still been alive.

Thanks to their heroism, Papa and Maman Ribouleau assured the future of our family.

When my grandchildren were growing up, I could not help but think of what would happen to them if their parents and grandparents were taken away. Who would volunteer to take them in their home, to feed them, to raise them, to love them? Who would accept such a responsibility, even in peacetime? They should never know the suffering that had been ours. To this day I often think of my cousin, Charlot, deported in 1944, brutally pushed in a train cattle car with one hundred other innocent people, children, women, and men, where he probably died of thirst or terror or trampled. If he survived the transport ordeal, he was either thrown in a burning pit or sent to the gas chamber on arrival in Auschwitz. For so many years, I had to hide my emotions when recollections of the war times surfaced. The memories at times were so intense, so real, so present, that I had to leave the room quickly and isolate myself so that nobody would see me crying.

In 1999, when I was sixty-one years old, I held an important position. As always, I loved my job and had never given any serious thought to retirement. During a yearly medical checkup the doctor, who was about my age and with whom I consulted yearly, told me that he would be retiring within a year. He asked me if I had considered retirement. I was surprised by his question and concerned at the same time.

"Is there a problem with my health?" I asked him nervously.

"No, no, Leon, at the contrary, you are in excellent health. However at our age, it is not possible to know how many good years we have ahead of us. You ought to think about slowing down, reducing progressively your professional activities and take advantage of your good health. Enjoy your family, your friends and the hobbies you always wanted to pursue but did not have the time to do so."

His recommendation made much sense. It was the trigger that led me to take my retirement at the age of sixty-two in 2000.

I did get used to the new life of retirement very quickly. I appreciated the freedom. I no longer had to fight the traffic to the office. I no longer had to be at the office at a given time. I no longer had to worry about all the issues associated with engineering and manufacturing problems. I no longer had to worry about the competition, the bookings of orders, the pressures of constantly increasing our sales, the people's problems. I did not even realize I was subject to such pressure until I stopped working. Several companies asked me to join their board of directors. It helped me stay in contact with the world of business and still feel useful by helping them to succeed with a lifelong business experience.

In 2003, on the promptings of a neighbor, I started cycling. At first, it was difficult and painful! It was a challenge to keep up with the group. I discovered that my old road bike was a lot heavier than the bikes my friends were riding. One of them lent me a lighter bike. What a difference! I quickly bought the latest and the greatest, and I made quick progress. My wife became an avid fan of the sport as well.

Besides cycling, I love to sail, ski and golf.

The days, the weeks, the months, the years go by at a rhythm that seems to accelerate every year. I am now more than twice the age of my parents when they were murdered. They remain young in my mind, the way they looked in the photos taken in their late twenties–early thirties.

The happiness that I enjoy is, somehow, a revenge for their tragic destiny.

Chapter 25

# The Righteous

In 1969 my sister Rachel and her husband Izzy traveled to Israel. As they were visiting the Yad Vashem Holocaust Memorial Museum in Jerusalem, they noticed a section entitled "The Righteous among the Nations." They had vaguely heard of the "Righteous" but had never given much attention to the significance of the word and certainly never knew that it could be so important to us. Interested, they asked for additional information. They learned that the title "Righteous among the Nations," taken from Talmud literature, had for generations been attributed to non-Jewish people with a positive, friendly attitude toward Jews and to anyone who has helped Jews, without looking for material compensation. They also learned that the State of Israel was still awarding the title of "Righteous among the Nations" to non-Jewish people who had risked their lives helping Jews in need during World War II. This honor was given based on the "word" of the survivors, eyewitness accounts, and reliable documentation.

Rachel looked at Izzy with excitement and cried out, "The Ribouleau are 'Righteous.' Let's find out how they can get this recognition while they are still alive."

They asked to meet with the Director of Yad Vashem. Rachel told her the story of our journey. The director explained the procedure. "Righteous Among the Nations" is an official title awarded by Yad Vashem on behalf of the State of Israel and the Jewish people to non-Jews who risked their lives to save Jews during the Holocaust. The title is awarded by a special commission headed by a Supreme Court Justice according to a well-defined set of criteria and regulations. The process could take several years. Given the age of Maman and Papa Ribouleau she promised to help speed up the process. That evening, Rachel called me, all excited about this wonderful news.

"There is an 'Avenue of the Righteous' at the Yad Vashem Museum in Jerusalem. Every person who has received the title of Righteous plants a tree there. Their name is engraved on a plaque at the foot of the tree. Can you imagine that the Ribouleaus would be immortalized?"

"Don't tell Papa and Maman Ribouleau about it yet," she added, the process can take several years."

"Rachel, that's great news. Finally, their courage and devotion will be officially recognized. Even after they are long gone, this tree and the plaque will remain there, forever." I said enthusiastically.

I was moved by this exciting possibility. I had hoped for a long time and worked hard for such courageous and wonderful people to be officially honored. I had tried to do so, without success, a number of times with the French government. How can we ever forget how these good neighbors we hardly knew who opened their door for us so generously, so bravely, without any conditions. What would have happened to us without these exceptional people? Who else would have so courageously risked their lives to take care of two Jewish children whom the invaders were hunting and wanted dead? Who would have fed two additional mouths for nearly three years during a time of deprivation, hardship, and denunciation, when most people were simply trying to survive and be inconspicuous. The Ribouleaus kept their word. They took care of us. They were exceptionally caring people. After the war, Maman Suzanne and Papa Henri rarely talked about their sacrifice and the danger they lived with as a result of their incredible action. During their lifetimes, when someone questioned them about their heroism during the occupation, they always replied with embarrassment, shyness and modesty "What we did was normal. We could not have done anything differently. We do not deserve any special thanks."

Two years after the application was submitted to the "Righteous" Commission, we were notified that the claim had been approved. The State of Israel recognized Maman and Papa Ribouleau as "Righteous among the Nations" on November 13, 1977. I called them immediately and shared this wonderful news.

There was an embarrassed silence at the other end of the line.

"Léon, that wasn't necessary. We really have not done anything extraordinary," said Papa Henri.

*Medal of the Righteous awarded to
Henri and Suzanne Ribouleau, 1978*

"No, nothing extraordinary," I said, my throat tightening up. "You only saved two children from deportation and certain death. You risked your lives and the lives of René and Marcel. You gave us the love and affection we needed. You shared your precious food with us, depriving yourselves and René and Marcel. You paid the rent for our parents' apartment for three years, convinced they would come back, and you say there was nothing extraordinary in what you have done?"

Studies have been conducted to understand the common traits of the Righteous. Some were religious and some were not. Some were involved with politics. Some had an altruistic character. Some might have had an adventurous spirit that encouraged them to fight and defy the murderous, apocalyptic Nazi madness. These studies have shown that many "Righteous" came from intellectual backgrounds. Some had developed friendly relations with Jewish neighbors, work colleagues and others before the war.

Interestingly, the Ribouleaus did not really fit in any of these categories.

They were simple, kind-hearted people who believed it was their duty to act the way they did, like helping someone in the street get up if they have fallen down. Obviously they lived in fear during the three years we were hidden in their home, afraid of being de-

*Suzanne Epelberg, friend of the family; Maman Suzanne, Papa Henri; Joseph Epelberg at the Israeli Consulate in Paris, 1978*

*Henri and Suzanne Ribouleau and the Israeli Consul in Paris, 1978*

nounced, afraid of starvation, afraid for their lives and the lives of their sons, afraid of not being able to find wood to cook and to heat the apartment, afraid of losing their jobs, and afraid of not being able to keep the promise to our parents to take care of us until their return.

We never felt that they regretted their action. We never felt we were a burden to the family.

The award of the "Medal of the Righteous" ceremony took place at the Israeli Consulate in Paris in October 1978.

Rachel and I were not present for this event. Catherine, Papa and Maman Ribouleau's granddaughter, Suzanne and Joseph Epelberg, close friends of our parents, represented both the Malmed and Ribouleau families. Shortly thereafter my sister and I invited Maman and Papa Ribouleau to Jerusalem. Marcel joined us. Rachel's youngest daughter, Hélène lived in Israel and worked in a kibbutz at the time. She was waiting for us at the Tel Aviv airport with her fiancé, Arie.

In September of 1979, we visited the Yad Vashem Memorial. Papa Henri was wearing his French "casquette." Maman Suzanne was dressed in a nice suit. They were both the image of goodness from a bygone era.

I loved watching them looking at this forest that they would soon become part of. We were silent out of respect for this symbolic place honoring so many families and the lives they saved.

Maman and Papa Ribouleau were very impressed. They were not used to being the focus of attention. They were uncomfortable in the hot sun dressed in their Sunday clothes. We slowly walked the Avenue of the Righteous, which was bordered on both sides with perfectly aligned trees, their shadow growing with each step. In front of each tree is a plaque with the name of the "Righteous" individual or family who saved one or more lives and the country where he, she or they lived during the war." We could see French, Dutch, Belgian names and others from many different European countries.

"In a few moments, your tree will be there as well," I tell Maman and Papa Ribouleau.

Rachel added, "The tree will grow with your names at its feet and the visitors will know what you have done for us and our descendants."

*Henri Ribouleau planting the tree at the Yad Vashem Memorial, 1979*

Papa Henri took off his cap out of respect for all those people who saved Jewish lives and for the people who were murdered. All were now immortalized by the living trees. We walked to the building where the ceremony was to take place. The French Consul, a rabbi, a cantor, and a few other personalities from the Yad Vashem Institute were waiting for us. The cantor began by singing a religious hymn. We formed a semicircle around a flame on the floor that symbolizes eternity. Maman Suzanne and Papa Henri stood very still, almost as if at attention. The room was charged with emotion. The rabbi read several prayers in French. I was holding Papa Henri and Maman Suzanne's hands tightly. I felt my parents' hands. I felt my cousin Charlot's small fingers clinging to mine. I felt my whole family, my uncles, aunts, and their children, all victims of the Nazi madness. Rachel and I were the family links between the living and the dead. We could hear, in our imagination, the loving voices and laughter of our parents. At a moment like this, it is difficult not to think of their suffering, the dread of not knowing about their children, their last thoughts before they died, the love they gave us and the joy we gave them for such a short time.

*Yad Vashem, Leon and the RighteousTree, 1982*

On that day we paid tribute to the people who allowed us to live. Rachel said a few words. Overwhelmed with emotion, I was speechless at that solemn time.

After the ceremony, we walked to the area where Papa Henri and Maman Suzanne would be planting the tree. A hole had been dug. Both of them positioned the small tree delicately and gently surrounded it with dirt. Marcel, Rachel, and I helped with the planting as well. The plaque with their names engraved was already in place.

It was a small young tree, like the young child I was when the Nazis stole my parents from me.

We were told that it was a "Carob," an eternal tree. We carefully poured water around it with the hope that the tree will grow and live a long time.

I turned to Maman Suzanne and asked her what she thought of this special occasion "Everything is wonderful and I thank everyone who has made this happen," she said. "It is a wonderful day. I thank the Consul and the personalities from the Memorial," Papa Henri added.

These few words were a simple reflection of their character.

This tiny tree, named after them, grew over the years. It embodies the kindness and generosity of these two remarkable people to whom our parents had entrusted their children, never knowing what happened to that engagement.

In their distress they would never know to what extent their neighbors had kept their promise. For my father who survived slavery and starvation for a couple of years, it must have been agony not knowing what happened to us. No doubt he would have been enormously relieved and at peace to have known that that this wonderful family had kept their word and saved us.

My parents undoubtedly died thinking about Rachel and me, never receiving the comfort and reassurance of knowing we were alive.

The Yad Vashem Institute team took pictures of all of us in front of the tree for the Museum archives. The ceremony ended with the Ribouleaus receiving an honorary diploma. Marcel was given a book in French about the Holocaust, as well as an insignia for himself and his brother René. René unfortunately couldn't come to the ceremony. Maman and Papa Ribouleau were asked to sign the "golden book."

As of January 1, 2012, 24,356 Righteous were recognized by the State of Israel.

We spent about a week traveling. We visited Jerusalem, Tel Aviv, Masada, the Dead Sea, the Sea of Galilee, the Golan and many religious sites. We went to the kibbutz where Hélène worked. Israel seemed so small compared to the vastness of America. The beaches are splendid. The streets were lively at almost any time of the day and late in the night. Café terraces were overflowing everywhere. The streets of Jerusalem are paved with stones extracted from surrounding quarries, the same quarries used for the construction of homes and buildings of many centuries ago. It is impressive to be in the Holy Land, the birthplace of three major monotheistic religions. So much history surrounded us.

Part of me has always stayed at Yad Vashem with that Carob tree, planted with Maman and Papa Ribouleau's hands. More than thirty years have gone by. That small tree has become a big tree reflecting the strength and courage they showed during the dark years of World War II.

The Talmud, the book of Jewish laws says "Whoever saves a life saves the entire world." This phrase is engraved on the medal that Catherine, their granddaughter, has preciously kept all these years.

Today, there are thirteen descendants of Srul and Chana Malmed.

Despite a powerful army with diabolical intentions, Hitler failed; the Nazis weren't able to exterminate us. We escaped the "Final Solution."

# Chapter 26

# Last Farewells

Years go by quickly.

In 1979, Papa Henri was seventy-eight and Maman Suzanne, seventy-three years old. My sister Rachel and I still kept exploring all possibilities to obtain further recognition for this courageous and generous couple.

I wrote to the President of France, Valery Giscard d'Estaing. I asked him to award the "Légion d'Honneur"* or an equivalent distinction to honor Papa and Maman Ribouleau.

I received a terse response from a local state administration office notifying me that the request had been denied.

"The deed fulfilled by the concerned parties, however remarkable, is too distant to receive a favorable opinion."

This form letter reply left me infuriated. Disappointed by such a lame excuse, I immediately responded:

"In a world devoid of morals and obligations towards other human beings, it seems to be your duty to recognize those, who by their actions, have given an example of heroism, courage, tenacity and honesty while risking their lives. It is inconceivable that France could have forgotten the events of World War II. It is impossible to think that France considers World War II so far-off a period of history and is not interested in the heroic deeds of its citizens. I am pleased to know that a great number of anonymous French citizens by their selfless behavior, without any material interest other than helping others in distress, have preserved the honor and the dignity of France."

This time the response came with a different pretext for turning down my request.

---

* The Légion d'Honneur is a French award created in 1802 by Napoleon Bonaparte. The order is the highest decoration bestowed to an individual by the nation.

"The Ribouleau do not come within the requirements of the "Légion d'Honneur" nor do they meet the requirements of the "l'Ordre du Mérite."† As to the "Medal for Acts of Courage and Dedication,"** this person quotes an excerpt of a government note indicating that a time limit is imposed for the award of this distinction for services rendered during the second World War: "If the granting of an honorific distinction at a time close to the events that have motivated the granting, it is no longer appropriate when this distinction is awarded after several years."

Despite the reasons cited to turn down my request, it was brought to my attention, a few years later, that the "Légion d'Honneur" was awarded to soldiers of World War I in early 2000 and to World War II American soldiers in 2011.

France is a country that has seen tremendous courage among its population. The French Resistance played a significant role during World War II, and suffered a great number of casualties. It is estimated that eight thousand underground fighters were killed in action, twenty-five thousand were shot by firing squad, and twenty-seven thousand were deported and died in extermination camps. In addition to the underground fighters casulties, about eighty-six thousand people, due to denunciations or being at the wrong place at the wrong time, were deported to extermination camps without racial motives, most of them accused of being terrorists.

Regretably, under the French government of "Pétain" many civil servants, at all levels, collaborated with the enemy. Some of these people participated, most of them not knowingly, in the murder of my parents as well as close to a hundred thousand of other innocents.

The civil servant of the nineteen seventies with whom I corresponded may have followed the example of his co-workers had he been employed in the early nineteen forties. He made the decision not to recognize and honor two courageous French citizens, who in a small way, saved the "French honor" by risking their lives and the lives of their two sons under the pretext that forty years have gone by.

---

* The National Order of Merit is awarded by the President of the French Republic. It is a lower award than the Légion d'Honneur.

† The Medal for Acts of Courage and Dedication is awarded for acts of devotion and acts of rescue.

What has happened to all the French police and other civil servants who have, by collaborating with the enemy, soiled the "French honor"? Were they ever asked why they collaborated? No, not that I am aware of. When the war was over, they probably continued in the same function and retired with a government pension as if the lives that they helped annihilate were only a detail in human history, quickly forgotten.

How can this person have determined this reward "too distant" and "without psychological interest?"

We had to wait another thirty years for the "French Righteous" to be recognized.

In January 2007 President Jacques Chirac unveiled a plaque at the Crypt of the Panthéon, a secular mausoleum in Paris, containing the remains of distinguished French citizens. He recognized two thousand six hundred French individuals who hid and saved Jews during World War II, the same individuals named "Righteous among the Nations" by the "Yad Vashem" memorial in Israel. This tribute underlines the fact that about three quarters of France's Jewish population survived the war, in most cases with the help of ordinary people like the Ribouleau family who provided help at the risk of their own lives.

This plaque says:

> "Under the cloak of hate and darkness that spread over France during the years of Nazi occupation, thousands of lights refused to be extinguished. Named as "Righteous among the Nations" or remaining anonymous, women and men, of all backgrounds and social classes, saved Jews from anti-Semitic persecution and the extermination camps. Braving the risks involved, they incarnated the honor of France and its values of justice, tolerance and humanity."

In 2008 the town of Compiègne also remembered Henri and Suzanne Ribouleau. A street was named after them. The street is located close to the Memorial of Internment and Deportation of the Royallieu camp.

Despite their courage and their goodness they were not immortal.

The first one to leave us was René, the older son of Papa Henri and Maman Suzanne. He retired from the French national railway company, in 1978. Almost ten years later, on October 23, 1987, he died following a long and painful illness. His death crushed Papa Henri and Maman Suzanne. They could not accept that their son had gone before them.

Papa's health was failing noticeably. I traveled to Europe two or three times a year and spent two or three days with them on each trip. Each visit, I found Papa Henri thinner and weaker. I noticed that he was always cold. Most of the time, he sat in the kitchen with his back touching the wall-mounted radiator. Each time I left to return home, I was afraid I would not see him alive again. Back in the States, I dreaded the inevitable phone call. I knew that Papa Henri was approaching the end of his life. We continued our correspondence. I had more and more difficulties reading his letters, his handwriting was deteriorating. The thought of not being able to say goodbye was heartbreaking. For a number of years I feared this ultimate and inescapable separation.

One day, I received a call from Marcel. His voice was shaky.

"Leon, he said, Papa is not well. He had a stroke last night."

"What do the doctors say?" I asked.

"They do not know. They say that he could recover. He is stable but he cannot speak. Hopefully he will improve," Marcel tells me.

I was speechless. I had a problem concentrating and coming up with further questions to help me decide if I should go to France now. I could not even voice some comforting thoughts. I was dazed. No, Papa Henri could not die. No.

I held the telephone by my ear but I had forgotten what it was for. It took me, what seemed minutes, before I recovered. Marcel was saying: "Leon, can you hear me? Leon..."

Finally, I told Marcel, "I will call Maman after we hang up. Thank you Marcel. Please kiss Papa and Maman for me."

I was all choked up.

I spoke to Maman after I regained composure. She did not have any additional information on Papa Henri's condition. It felt good to hear her voice.

I called her back the next morning. The news was good. She said in a cheerful voice. "Do not worry, Leon, Papa is much better; he is strong and he is recuperating fast."

A few days later he was back home and spoke almost normally. What a relief!

Two months went by and I got another call from Marcel:

"Papa had another stroke. According to the doctors, this one is very serious. He is in a coma."

"I am coming. I want to see him alive," I told Marcel with emotion.

The next day, Patricia and I were on our way to France. As soon as we got to Compiègne, we went from the airport directly to the hospital. Papa Henri was lying on his back, eyes opened and fixed, not seeing anything probably. The nurse told us that he could hear us, but we could not tell if he did or not.

I took his hand gently and told him, "Papa, it's Leon and Patricia."

No reaction. I did not want to show him my desperation, just in case he could see or hear us. Patricia was on the other side of the bed. She also had enormous affection for Papa Henri and vice versa. As a former nurse, she had seen a number of dying patients and was more armored than I was, but she could not hold her tears. We spent the evening and a good part of the night with him, hoping that he would give us a sign of recognition. I kept holding his hand hoping that he would squeeze it even so slightly. Nothing happened. We hoped naively that our presence would wake him up from his comatose state. We wanted to believe the nurse. Before we left, Patricia was holding his hand and thinks that she felt a slight squeeze. Both of us were now crying. He heard us!

We left late that night. It was so difficult to leave.

The next morning when we came back we were told that he had

passed away shortly after we left. Had he waited for us before leaving this world?

We knew of his inescapable death. It still was extremely painful.

We were with him almost to the end. So many memories poured out. I was overwhelmed by grief.

We helped organize the funeral. The religious service was held in the Catholic Church called "Eglise de la Victoire." The church was too small to accomodate the family and all the friends who had come. It spilled outside through the wide opened doors. The town Mayor and Senator attended and eulogized Papa Henri. I also spoke; I paid my last respects to the man who was my wonderful second father for decades. I did not know if I would be able to go through my address. I asked my niece, Frédérique, the great granddaughter of Papa Henri and Maman Suzanne to be next to me in case I would need help to finish my allocution. With a few hesitations I was able to go through. At the cemetery, I saluted for the last time, the man, so honest, so courageous to whom I owed my life.

He was eighty-one years old.

What was going to happen to Maman Suzanne? Would she be able to live in this big house by herself?

After our return to the States, I called her several times a week for years. She missed Papa Henri enormously.

In 1990, she decided to leave her home where she had lived forty years. She moved to an assisted living facility, close to the Castle of Compiègne. It was very difficult at first for her to get used to a very small apartment in a building with people she had little in common, except for their age. Slowly, she began to make friends and to like her situation. She seemed relatively happy when I talked to her on the phone and visited with her. She spent most of her days knitting blankets for the benefit of charities.

To celebrate her ninetieth birthday, Marcel, Rachel and I organized a family reunion in a restaurant located in "Vieux-Moulin," a hamlet close to Compiègne. It happened to be the same village where Rachel and I stayed at the home of the Baron of Rothschild shortly after the end of the war to prevent further problems with our Uncle and Aunt Blum.

The Malmed and Ribouleau families were together once more. Papa Henri and René were missing. Corinne, our daughter and her husband came from the U.S. to be with all of us. It was a wonderful celebration. Daniel Meyers,* an American film maker, had also come from the U.S. with a small team to realize a documentary about the Ribouleau family. He used the day's footage in his Documentary "17 rue Saint Fiacre."

Patricia and I went to get Maman Suzanne at the retirement home and bring her to the restaurant. She was smartly dressed and looked very happy. On the way, we stopped at the "Etangs de Saint Pierre," two small beautiful lakes in the middle of the forest to reminisce our fishing expeditions during and after the war. Maman Suzanne was smiling. She was, however, showing some signs of Alzheimer's. She was a bit confused and had a hard time recognizing people.

When we entered the restaurant, she was received with long and warm applause. She was surprised and embarrassed by the attention. There were many toasts and speeches dedicated to her during the delicious meal. Rachel and I thanked her and Marcel as well as (in absentia) Papa Henri and René, for having saved our lives and enabled the Malmed family to survive.

That evening, my sister asked me:

"Did you notice that Maman Suzanne has trouble recognizing people?"

"Yes, Marcel had talked to me about it. I am afraid that she is at the beginning of a long decline. It is a terrible thought!" I said.

On my next visits, I noted how fast the disease was progressing. In 1996, she could no longer live in the assisted living facility. Marcel, himself fighting cancer, found a nursing home in the center of the town. She could hardly walk and was able to recognize only a very few people.

A year later, June 2nd, 1987, Marcel passed away. Patricia and I flew to France a few days earlier when we were told of his condition. We were at his bedside when he died.

It is painful to see the people we love leave forever. My respect, my love for this family will be with me as long as I live.

The Alzheimer's desease was now completely isolating Maman Suzanne from normal life. Her speech had deteriorated to the point

---

* Daniel Meyers, a California native, produced a 24-minute documentary entitled "17 rue St. Fiacre" (The National Center for Jewish Film, 1999); see Chapter 27.

of not being understandable. She did not realize that Marcel had died. Perhaps, it was better that way. Curiously, she recognized me almost to the end.

In 1998, Catherine, Marcel's daughter called me:

"Grandma is not well. The doctor thinks that she only has a few days, a week maximum."

"Tell her that I am coming, Catherine," I said to her, knowing that Maman would not understand.

Again, I was hanging to the hope that I would still be able to speak to her. Corinne, our daughter who lived in the U.S., and my cousin Salomon from Lyon joined us at the bedside of Maman Suzanne.

As children, Corinne and Olivier loved to go and spend their summer vacations with Papa and Maman Ribouleau. They went fishing with Papa Henri and Marcel. Maman Suzanne was an excellent cook, and she would prepare for them delicious meals and desserts. At night, they would all sit outside and talk while observing the moon, the stars and look for the first few satellites in the sky.

Maman Suzanne lived another week after we arrived in Compiègne. We stayed with her all the time. We talked to her with the hope that she might hear us. I told her about the good memories, the times we had enjoyed together and the difficult moments we had known together.

She was taken care of by a wonderful nurse. She was lying on her bed, unconscious, dying, eyes open without comprehension, a brain no longer able to find its way among the ruptured threads of her impaired memory.

On October 15, 2003, she passed away peacefully.

Patricia, Corinne, Daniel, René's son, Sali and I were with her at the moment she exhaled her last breath.

A long chapter of my life had just ended.

We stayed a long time in the room where she was resting, crying and hugging each other. We were deeply saddened by Maman's death.

I spoke again at the religious service to a large audience that had come to pay their last respects to this exceptional woman and exceptional family, whose life could be summarized in few words: selfless, loving, self sacrificing, and courageous. I said, "Rachel and I have had two mothers. The first one has given us life. The second one has saved our lives. Both of them had something in common: they loved us dearly." I recalled the arrest of our parents and their promise to them, the first time I dared calling them Papa and Maman and looking for their reaction, the roundups, our escape through the fields, the hunger and the fear we had endured together for three years. Then I addressed my departed Maman Suzanne.

"I remember your kindness, your generosity, your affection, your advices and your love. I remember how hard you worked for all of us, your weekends in the basement washing by hand our clothes and beddings and how heavy the bed sheets were when I helped you throw them over the garden wire to dry. I remember the rare moments of relaxation you enjoyed when you knitted sweaters, hats and more. I remember the day, in 1944, at lunch time, when you arrived breathless, screaming for me to leave as the Gestapo was turning the corner of our street one hundred yards away, coming to pick us up along with the last few remaining Jewish children in town. I will remember your sacrifices, always."

Each of these memories was like a knife stabbing and tearing at my heart. It was so difficult to accept that the last link of this family made out of courage and love, a family that had saved us, my sister Rachel and me, from a certain and atrocious end, was gone forever.

Despite the support of Patricia and the whole family, I felt very lonely in this world for a while. For the second time in my life, I was an orphan.

The heroes of our overwhelming and so tragic life story were gone forever, but they will never be forgotten.

Beyond the Malmed family, it is the soul of humanity that the Ribouleaus have preserved.

Chapter 27

# Pass on the Memory

In August 1995, my sister met by chance an American filmmaker, Daniel Meyers. After he heard our story, he volunteered to produce a documentary about the Ribouleau family.

Daniel Meyer's mother was French. She lived in Paris during the war. On July 16 and 17, 1942, the days of the infamous Vel' d'Hiv' (Vélodrome d'Hiver) roundup, she was on the list to be arrested. When the Germans, accompanied by the French police, came to take her away, the concierge of her apartment building hid her in her kitchen closet. She survived the war. The concierge was recognized as a Righteous among the Nations by the State of Israel.

Daniel was aware of the Righteous as a result of his mother's experience. He participated in the Steven Spielberg project* to collect as many Shoah† survivors' testimonies as possible. Daniel shared with my sister Rachel and me how emotional it was for him to film these documentaries.

---

* In 1994, Steven Spielberg founded the Survivors of the Shoah Visual History Foundation, an organization established to record testimonies of survivors and other witnesses of the Holocaust. Between 1994 and 1999 the Foundation conducted 52,000 interviews in 56 countries and in 32 languages. Interviewees included Jewish survivors, Jehovah's Witness survivors, homosexual survivors, liberators and liberation witnesses, political prisoners, rescuers and aid providers, Roma survivors, and war crimes trials participants.

† The biblical word *shoah*, meaning "calamity," became the standard Hebrew term for the Holocaust in the 1940s. The word *holocaust* is from the Greek: "whole" and "burnt." In Hebrew: HaShoah, "catastrophe, "destruction" was the genocide of approximately six million European Jews during World War II. Of the nine million Jews who had resided in Europe before the Holocaust, approximately two-thirds, including over one million Jewish children, two million Jewish women, and three million Jewish men, were murdered in the Holocaust. The Nazis used a euphemistic phrase, the "Final Solution to the Jewish Question" (German: Endlösung der Judenfrage). Nazis also used the phrase "lebensunwertes Leben" (life unworthy of life) in an attempt to justify the killings.

He was interested in producing one as a tribute to the Ribouleau family. We accepted his generous proposal. Rachel and I met Daniel and his team in France. It was the first time we had participated in such a project. Daniel Meyers produced the documetary entitled "17 rue Saint Fiacre." This documentary was shown at numerous film festivals.

When I reached the age of 65, I felt that I had a duty to share the events I had lived. Suddenly, it became urgent to pass on and preserve the memories. I quickly made arrangements to interview two cousins, Jacques Malmed and Jean Gerbaez, as well as my only living aunt, Sarah Blum. The three of them were the only family left who were born in Poland. Their testimony helped me a great deal to understand and rebuild our family history.

In 2003, on the sixtieth anniversary of the Holocaust, the Jewish community of Savannah, Georgia, where our daughter lives, invited me to speak as a survivor. There were five hundred attendees. A number of people approached me afterward and asked if I had written a book. I was getting that question more and more often as I talked about the Holocaust to students in schools and adults in churches and synagogues. Many of my friends kept asking "Why don't you write a book? You owe it to your children and the millions who died and cannot speak about the horrors they endured. The World needs to know what happened to all of you."

I was surprised that the few pages I had written stirred up so much interest. For a long time, I thought these people were simply being kind and compassionate.

Writing more than the eight to ten pages I had put together about our difficult journey during the war seemed almost impossible. Other than a number of speeches I had written for work, writing any long document—let alone a book—felt like a monumental task. I could not see how I could restore all the memories with the limited information I had at the time, due to the death of so many family members and friends of the family. Many witnesses had passed away, their memories buried with them. Only these two cousins, an aunt, my sister and myself were still alive. I had kept silent all this time trying to forget about the tragedy. My work kept me very busy. I traveled more than fifty percent of the time worldwide. I came up with so many unacceptable excuses to justify not undertaking the difficult task of writing this book.

When Papa Henri, Maman Suzanne, René, and Marcel were alive, I never asked questions about our parents, the family they saw, their friends, and their habits. I did not want to bother them by rehashing sad memories. I deeply regret it. I found it nearly impossible to bring up the subject. It was also too emotional. Looking back, it was my way of distancing myself from the tragedy.

I wanted to look at the future and close the door on those painful memories. How can I ever forget? I thought I could. At the same time, I just could not see myself starting a conversation by saying, "Can we talk about our life during the war?" Why not?

Even with my children, I was not able to break the silence. I only mentioned in broad strokes the arrest of our parents and the years of hiding. They were and still are shy about asking questions. They probably were concerned about hurting my feelings for the same reasons that I did not ask questions. Perhaps they think that they know enough? Or are those events so far back that their current preoccupations take precedent? I doubt it.

As for the new generations, the tragic events of World War II are ancient history. They may find it interesting if they were to hear about it from people who have witnessed it. It is difficult if not impossible for anyone to imagine that such barbarism and quest for power could have taken place.

My sister has also begged me to write this book for many years. Each time we talked to each other, once or twice a week, she would ask me with urgency in her voice: "So, have you started writing?" I'd answer no. "When, Leon. When? You must do it before it is too late." She spoke about the Holocaust for many years in schools, churches and synagogues. I finally decided to follow in her footsteps and accepted invitations by similar organizations.

During the summer of 2007, while visiting with my sister in New York, we sat and talked about our childhood. I was taking notes on a yellow pad. We were surprised at how many memories were surfacing. People we had known when we were children and we had forgotten about were coming back to life. Scenes we had not thought of for years were also coming back to life. Who knows, maybe some of these people were still alive?

Following this visit, I wrote about fifty pages in English. I started to spend many hours on the phone trying to locate people in France I thought may have known our family before and during the war—our neighbors, friends of the family, our schoolteachers, our schoolmates and anyone who would be able to provide information of that period. Anyone who would be able to jog my memory, fill the gaps and talk about the events of those days, of which I was unaware or had forgotten, was of interest.

The grandchildren of Papa and Maman Ribouleau, Catherine and Daniel Ribouleau still live in Compiègne. They helped me with the research as well. Slowly, the pieces of the puzzle that I thought could never be completed were coming together. The daughter of a longtime Parisian friend introduced me to a friend of hers who happened to be a resident of Compiègne. She is a college professor of French literature. She has published several books, some about the internment camps and the Holocaust. I needed an editor and she was the ideal person to help me. After having read the first fifty pages I had written in English, she offered to help me if I were to write the book in French. I accepted. My rusty French needed to be tuned up. Close to six years have passed since I undertook this emotional trip into the past. The documents have piled up. The memories have come back, some precise as they happened recently and some fuzzy. The pages have filled up.

I have been able to retrace important events of my childhood and to resurrect, in some way, my parents who left this world too early under such inhuman conditions. I often cried as I typed and had to stop until my vision cleared up. I was able to totally isolate myself from the present and transport myself sixty plus years back. It was like being in a trance. Many times I was so involved in my thought process that I could feel the departed close to me. I could imagine hearing their voices, voices I had never heard, voices that were mute for more than sixty years.

Should I ever close the curtain? Certainly not. My foray in the past has left me, at times, exhausted. A strong impetus has driven me to complete this book in French and then in English. Although I had hoped that revisiting the past and recounting it would have freed me, somehow, of the heavy burden that I have carried all my life. But it has not as yet totally and probably never will.

I will never be able to forgive and certainly to forget the crimes committed toward my parents, my family, my sister, and me. I probably will remain behind this fictional partition with my family whose young lives were savagely terminated. I could never abandon them.

With time, the events take a different dimension. It is like a painting which is often better appreciated from a certain distance. I was hardly five years old when I was engulfed in the torment of the war. But unlike a painting, it is impossible to step back far enough to perceive the full impact of the inhumane brutal separation from one's parents. It took me more than half a century to face the past and relive it. It took me two and half years to complete the writing of the French version and another two years to rewrite it in English.

I will always feel a deep sense of injustice and find it impossible to comprehend the motivation for such tragic events.

I hoped for decades that my parents would come back. It was extremely difficult to accept that I would never see them again. I hung on to the hope that some deportees had suffered from amnesia as a result of torture and the savage treatments they had been submitted to, and others had been taken to Siberia. They could come back.

A friend of mine, Doctor Eva Tichauer, survived three years in Auschwitz. She has written a book based on her experience entitled *J'étais le numéro 20832 à Auschwitz* ("I was number 20832 in Auschwitz"). A few years back, she subscribed me to a newspaper *Le Patriote Résistant*. The articles are often accompanied with photos of the concentration camps. With the insane hope of recognizing my parents, I used a magnifying glass to look at the pictures.

Writing this book has helped me, but has not completely freed me of the anguish I have felt when I think of the war. I hope to find some peace when it is completed. I am impatient for my children, grandchildren, and family to read it. They will acquire a better understanding of the sequels of wars and of the family they have been deprived of.

Soon this narrative will come to an end. It has allowed me to come out of my shell; to break the silence and the self-imposed taboo. I was able to overcome the emotions that have prevented me, for such a long time, from openly recalling my childhood. It was time, at the age of seventy, to pass on the memory to other generations. I am accomplishing the ultimate mission of "Passeur" (Courrier). The memories of the Malmed and Ribouleau families will be kept forever.

I also hope that writing about my personal story and related events that took place sixty years ago, events that could have annihilated the world, will contribute modestly to a better world.

*Is this a utopian thought?*

Fortunately, the "good guys" won the war. There are still many, unfortunately, on this earth who continue to perpetrate ethnic and religious hatred.

I have chosen to write about not only the tragedies of the war but also of the ways I have reconstructed my life. My existence, as chaotic as it was early on, has eventually transformed itself into a happy life. The hardships I have been submitted to, rather than destroying me, have helped me appreciate life. I do hope that my own experiences will help young people in doubt about their future or who are facing difficulties.

What I lived through during the war pales in comparison to the horrors of the extermination camps. I was lucky to avoid the round-ups and subsequent death. I was very fortunate to survive, protected by exceptionally generous and courageous people. Because of the example of such people, I was able to overcome the past without being dragged backwards. When in personal and business life, I was confronted with difficult issues, I thought of the fate of my parents. It helped me resolve problems that seemed unsolvable. I am so lucky to be alive.

At the age of thirteen, when I was separated from my sister and living in an environment I despised, I decided to rebel and change the course of my life. I met this challenge by seeking help from people I trusted and felt could help me. I was able to convince adults to trust me as well. This victory, at a critical time in my life, has helped me to reject the status quo and to try no matter how bleak the outcome seems to be. After this early experience, I was convinced that I could overcome the obstacles I would encounter on the way to adulthood. That is how I built my future.

What I am today, I have earned it by my desire to constantly improve myself and everything and everyone around me, to learn, to discover, to listen and to respect other people's thinking. I have avoided the bitterness that could have destroyed me. I did not seek revenge on those who have murdered my parents and stolen my childhood. I did not feel sorry for myself about the past. I probably inherited these traits from my parents and was reinforced with Papa and Maman Ribouleau. They taught me that generosity, persistence, honor, and being trusted were the real values of life.

Despite the horrors committed by humans, the massacres that

are still perpetuated today, I remain optimistic. Man possesses unsuspected resources of goodness, generosity, and courage.

Alas, history repeats itself. It seems that humanity keeps falling, on a regular basis, into the chaos of wars and conflicts. We need to rejoice that the Nazis assassins were vanquished. But at what price to the democratic nations?

Some people hang on to religious beliefs and look for spiritual guidance to give them the comfort we all need. I do believe that good always triumphs if each of us makes a contribution to stamp out evil.

I return to Compiègne regularly. My roots are there. I like the town, its people, its environment, its forest, its castles, its churches, its monuments, its town hall, and the villages surrounding it. Everything is familiar. Even though I knew years of fear and deprivation there, I have also known the love of a close knit family. I still meet people from my generation. I have stayed close to Papa and Maman Ribouleau's grandchildren and great grandchildren to this day. I make more friends on each visit. The name "Ribouleau" is well known and respected in Compiègne. Every time I return there, I always pay a visit to "rue St Fiacre" and stop in front of number 17. The building was purchased a few years ago by a young couple who have transformed it into a beautiful bed and breakfast. These wonderful people have insisted that we be their guests in that home so full of my memories. There, I close my eyes and revisit my childhood. The images are moving fast. I see the neighbors, the children playing in the street, excited, red cheeks, the florist, the employee of the PTT, the woman across the street who fraternized with a German soldier, the *Père Lapinpeaux* in his horse carriage who bought our rabbit skins, the butcher, the radio repairman, the gendarmes who took my parents away, the trucks with the SS soldiers coming to arrest us. No one has aged.

In 2009, I went to Auschwitz, encouraged by my cousin Salomon, who had made the trip the year before. This ultimate pilgrimage was difficult. I went to Auschwitz the same way we go to a cemetery to meditate on a grave. I had hoped that I would find a trace of our parents' stay, a picture, a date, a name, a witness so that I would feel their presence.

After the visit, I knew that they were gone forever.

At last I could start the mourning.

# Chapter 28

# The Pilgrimage

I saw Auschwitz-Birkenau, the symbol of crimes against humanity.

Today, I know. I have no more doubts. For many years I lived in limbo with the absurd hope that my parents might have survived. For decades I carried the heavy burden of doubt. Now that I have seen the Auschwitz-Birkenau and other extermination camps in Poland, I know.

I had refused to accept the reality for too long. It was impossible for me to envision that such barbarism, brutality, cruelty, inhumaity could have taken place. It was impossible to believe that a genocide on that scale happened in the twentieth century.

Movies, documentaries, photos and articles cannot describe in its full dimension the horror we can feel and almost see when visiting these places. I have seen the chimneys of the ovens that reduced innocent human beings, men, women, and children to ashes.

I did not smell the burning flesh like the millions of deportees to the death camps had.

Who would have believed that a cultivated, civilized nation could have carried out such sadistic and murderous madness?

Who would have believed that a nation of engineers, physicists, writers, musicians, and intellectuals could set in place an infrastructure designed specifically to exterminate on an industrial scale millions of innocent and decent human beings?

The deceit was so well engineered that it was impossible for the deportees to know what awaited them when they arrived at the death camp.

I have walked by the railroad tracks where my parents were unloaded from the death train and greeted by the torturers with their killer dogs. Those railroad tracks that brought millions of dead, half dead, men and women, some pregnant, children, and old people. They had been jam-packed, one hundred or more per railroad car

*Ashes of hundreds of thousands of children, women, and men murdered at the Majdanek (Poland) extermination camp.*

that was designed to transport eight horses. They stood for three to five days until they collapsed or died of exhaustion, thirst, or suffocation. They were Jews, underground combatants, and unlucky people, my parents among them, without water, hygiene, food, nor the possibility to sit or lie down. I saw the train platform where my parents, if my mother were still alive, were brutally forced to jump from the cattle cars in the midst of barking, biting German shepherds, trained to kill, and equally savage SS soldiers yelling incomprehensible orders and hitting the deportees with their whips and rifle butts filling their murderous need.

I saw the "Selection" dock where most of the new arrivals were selected and taken immediately to the gas chambers and ovens where up to twelve thousand innocents were reduced to ashes each day.

I saw the mountain of ashes at the Majdanec extermination camp, the remains of millions of people, victims of the worst crimes humanity ever witnessed. In this concentration camp, the wife of the commandant manufactured lampshades with the skin of deportees she had ordered skinned. For entertainment she would have deportees thrown alive in the huge kennel where they were shredded and devoured by the German shepherds being trained to kill.

I saw the pond, in Auschwitz-Birkenau, with the gray bottom where the ashes of hundreds of thousands, perhaps millions, of murdered innocent human beings rest. Are the ashes of my parents in that pond?

I saw a pathway half a mile long going from the Birkenau camp to the "farms," where two farmhouses stood. The SS had installed the first gas chambers connected to the exhaust pipes of large trucks. In July 1942, the two rigged gas chambers were insufficient for the mass extermination of deportees arriving every day from all over Europe. The SS had devised an alternate ignominious means of murdering on a mass scale.

They formed an alley about three hundred yards long from the area the deportees selected to die were waiting to go to their new destination. Spacing themselves on each side, a few feet from each other, the SS forced the deportees to run, naked, while whipping them and with their rifle butts urging them toward a clearing next to the farms where they were pushed alive in a pit burning permanently fueled by human flesh.

My parents were part of the first mass transports to Auschwitz in July 1942. I fear that my mother, if she survived the trip from Drancy to Auschwitz, might have left this world this way.

I saw the mounds of shoes, of clogs, of toys, of hair in the barracks at Auschwitz.

Hair was shaved from all the deportees before the "shower," alias gas chamber. Hair was converted into fabric by the German clothing and furniture industry.

How is it possible that so many German engineers, chemists, doctors, physicists, manufacturing specialists could have ignored the origin of the human parts they were directed to convert into industrial products? Of course they knew! All of them were as criminal as their SS compatriots.

I saw the barracks built to accommodate a hundred people in which a thousand deportees were crowded, six per bunk, and only enough toilets and wash basins for one hundred.

After a twelve-hour workday under horrendous conditions, hot summers and extremely cold winters, they would be given greasy water with a moldy piece of bread.

How can one devise such bestiality, such sadism, such cruelty?

How can the German army, their allies, and so many civilians agree to participate in such crimes?

Is it possible to hope for human behavior to change?

I am convinced that the Red Cross representatives were aware of what was happening in the extermination camps. They could not have been duped this much. They knew about the atrocities as early as August 1942. To save face and to give themselves a good conscience, they visited a few camps set up by the Nazis as model camps, such as Theresienstadt (Terezin, Czech Republic). The deportees were ordered to build an artificial village, aka Disney Land. They were fed properly for a few days prior to the Red Cross visit. They were dressed smartly the day of the visit. The deportees had no knowledge of the deception, as they thought that it would last. The day after the visit, they were all exterminated.

The European and the American heads of State as well as the religious authorities knew about the extermination camps and the atrocities. No action was taken to stop or to slow down the slaughter. For years, they remained silent while the ashes of innocents were fertilizing the German fields.

Some excerpts of historical records:

In October 1941, the Assistant Chief of the U.S. delegation to the Vatican, Harold Tittman, asked the Pope to condemn the atrocities. The response came that the Holy See wanted to remain "neutral," and that condemning the atrocities would have a negative influence on Catholics in German-held lands.

November 24, 1942 — U.S. State Department confirms the existence of Nazi extermination camps and the murder of two million Jews to date. Rabbi Stephen Wise holds press conference in New York to announce that the Nazis were deporting Jews throughout German-occupied territory to Poland for mass slaughter. The news makes little impact as the next day's *New York Times* reported this news on the tenth page. Throughout the rest of the war the *N.Y. Times* and most other newspapers failed to give prominent and extensive coverage to the Holocaust.

December 8, 1942 — Jewish leaders meet with President Roosevelt and handed him a 20-page summary of the Holocaust.

December 17, 1942 — The Allies issue a statement condemning "in the strongest possible terms this bestial policy of cold-blooded extermination."

January 1943 — U.S. State Department receives information from Switzerland that discloses that 6,000 Jews a day are being killed at one location in Poland.

February 10, 1943 — U.S. State Department asks legation in Switzerland to discontinue sending reports about the mass murder of Jews to private persons in the U.S.

To my knowledge, none of these people in positions to denounce the Holocaust early on were ever questioned about their silence and behavior as to this monstrous genocide.

As Emile Zola* said in 1898 in his letter to the French authorities regarding the Dreyfus Affair, when Captain Dreyfus, a man of Jewish faith, was falsely accused of treason, "J'ACCUSE."

Now, it is my turn to "ACCUSE" (blame) all the Heads of State, Civil and Religious. They have contributed, by remaining silent, to the murders of millions of men, women and children. They could have, if not prevented totally the genocide, denounced it publicly, and by doing so, limited its magnitude.

Could my parents, more than half of my family and millions of others who were savagely assassinated, have been saved if those in charge of the world and its religions had not remained silent?

They bear responsibility. It is incomprehensible that none of them publicly and forcefully denounced the ongoing mass murder for close to three years.

In June 1939 nine hundred and eight Jewish refugees seeking asylum from Nazi persecution left Hamburg for Cuba by boarding the ship *Saint-Louis*, a German ocean liner. Captain Schröder, a non-Jewish German citizen, went to great lengths to ensure dignified treatment for the passengers. The Cuban government admitted 22 Jewish passengers. The remaining passengers were turned down. The ship sailed towards the U.S., hoping that the United States would allow the passengers to disembark and provide asylum. They

---

* French author Émile Zola (1840-1902) wrote the influential article "J'accuse" (I blame!), an open letter to French president Félix Faure accusing the French government of anti-Semitism. It was published on the front page of the Paris newspaper *L'Aurore* (*The Dawn*) on 13 January 1898 in response to the suppression of evidence of the innocence of Captain Alfred Dreyfus, a Jewish officer in the French army, hastily tried and convicted of treason in 1894 and condemned to life imprisonment at a penal institution in Guyana. He was rehabilitated in 1906 after the discovery of fabricated evidence by the military establishment.

sailed so close to Florida that the passengers could see the lights of Miami, but the White House did not permit the refugees to enter the United States. On June 6, 1939, the ship returned to Europe. Two hundred eighty-eight passengers were allowed to disembark in England. The others disembarked in Holland, Belgium, and France. Of the 620 passengers who returned to Europe, 87 managed to emigrate before the German invasion of Western Europe in May 1940, but 532 of the *Saint-Louis* passengers were trapped when Germany conquered Western Europe. Of these, 278 survived the Holocaust. Of the 254 who were exterminated by the Nazis, 84 had been in Belgium, 84 in Holland, and 86 had been admitted to France. The well-publicized refusal by the United States and other countries to provide asylum to these people fleeing persecution was a boost to Hitler's plan to exterminate entire civilizations.

In Auschwitz-Birkenau, there is a room describing in detail the make-up of all the convoys. Each train transported about one thousand deportees to the slaughterhouse. The convoys consisted of ten railroad cattle cars. One hundred or more deportees were crammed in each car, preventing people from being able to sit or lie down. Each railroad car was locked from the outside at the departure point and unlocked at destination three to five days later.

Thirty percent of the deportees died during the transport, from being trampled on, from thirst, asphyxia, madness, or other sickness.

I often think of the three or four days my parents and their unfortunate companions spent on the train to Hell.

I now know where they died. It is impossible to fully understand the nightmare they lived. I have walked in the places they had been and seen some of what they saw before life was taken away from them.

How can I feel at peace? How can I forgive? How can I accept? How can I forget?

Forgetting would be equivalent to accepting.

If we look at history through a rearview mirror, we know that human beings have been fighting each other for more than three thousand years. I wish from the depth of my heart that this testimony inspires some people to contribute to world peace.

I was eight years old in 1945 when I was told that the United Nations would prevent any more wars. What a beautiful name "The

United Nations." So promising ... In the end, so disappointing.

I pay tribute to all the unknown French citizens who resisted the occupation at the risk of their lives and that of their families and friends. I pay tribute to those people who, for close to four years, lived night and day in fear of being denounced, being arrested, being tortured and dying at the hands of a savage enemy.

I pay tribute to the thousand of soldiers of the Allied forces and their families, who, by their sacrifice and their courage, freed Europe of the Nazi monstrosity and allowed my sister and me to live. I pay tribute to the thousands of unknown heroes who were not recognized for their bravery.

I pay tribute to all those who never shared with their family and friends the heroics of their sacrifice and of their actions in a mad era for fear of embarrassing them. Many like me were not able to control their emotion when the horrible memories resurfaced.

At last, I decided to testify with the hope that my children, my grandchildren, my friends, and the readers would prevent, in their very small way, repeating the mistakes of the past.

# Appendix:

# Family

| | |
|---|---|
| Srul Malmed | Leon Malmed's father |
| Chana Malmed | Leon Malmed's mother |
| Rivka Packer Malmed (Boubé) | Leon Malmed's grandmother |
| | |
| Sylviane Malmed | Leon Malmed's first spouse |
| Olivier Malmed | Leon Malmed's son |
| Corinne Lee | Leon Malmed's daughter |
| | |
| Patricia Malmed | Leon Malmed's spouse |
| James Malmed | Leon Malmed's son |
| | |
| Jacques Malmed | Leon Malmed's cousin |
| Salomon Malmed | Leon Malmed's cousin |
| Gela Kibel | Salomon's mother |
| | |
| Rachel Epstein-Malmed | Leon Malmed's sister |
| Izzy Epstein | Rachel's husband |
| | |
| Henri Ribouleau | Saved Leon and Rachel |
| Suzanne Ribouleau | Saved Leon and Rachel |
| René Ribouleau | Son of Henri and Suzanne |
| Marcel Ribouleau | Son of Henri and Suzanne |
| Gilberte Ribouleau | Marcel's wife |
| Daniel Ribouleau | Son of René Ribouleau |
| Catherine Ribouleau | Daughter of Marcel Ribouleau |
| | |
| Charles Blum | Leon's uncle, Chana's brother |
| Sarah Blum | Leon's aunt, Srul's sister |
| | |
| Idah Gerbaez | Leon's Aunt, Srul's sister |
| Jean Gerbaez | Leon's cousin, Idah's son |
| George Gerbaez | Leon's cousin, Idah's son |
| Maurice Gerbaez | Leon's cousin, Idah's son |
| | |
| Marcel Clausse | Neighbor on the first floor |
| Yolande Clausse | Marcel Clausse's wife |

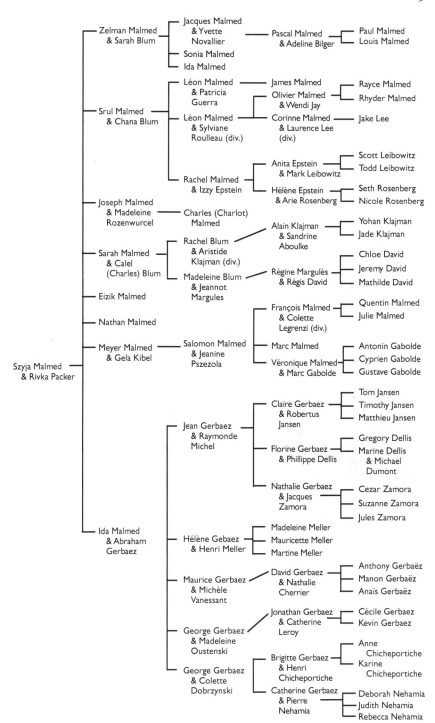

## About the Author

Leon Malmed was born in 1937 in Compiègne,
France. He emigrated to the United States in 1964,
and worked in the High-Tech industry in Silicon
Valley. He currently lives in California
with his wife.

The University of Nebraska–Lincoln does not discriminate
based on gender, age, disability, race, color,
religion, marital status, veteran's status,
national or ethnic origin,
or sexual orientation.